AUGUST STRINDBERG (1849-1912) is best known outside Sweden as a dramatist, the author of the great Naturalistic dramas *Miss Julie* and *The Father*, and of the pioneering Expressionist dramas *To Damascus* and *A Dream Play*. But he was also a prolific writer of novels, short stories, essays, journalism and poetry, as well as being a notable artist and photographer. Although he spent many years abroad, Strindberg was born, grew up and died in Stockholm.

AGNES BROOMÉ is a native of Sweden, but has spent the last ten years in the UK, studying linguistics and comparative literature. She is currently working on a PhD in literary sociology at UCL where she also teaches Swedish-English translation.

ANNA HOLMWOOD is a literary translator from Chinese and Swedish. She was chosen in 2010 for the British Centre for Literary Translation's mentorship scheme and has since translated two novels and countless short stories for publication.

JOHN K MITCHINSON completed all levels of his higher education at UCL: a BA in German and Scandinavian Studies, an MA in Advanced Scandinavian Translation and, most recently, a PhD in Scandinavian Linguistics. He currently teaches Swedish and Faroese at the university.

MATHELINDA NABUGODI is a PhD student in Comparative Literature at University College London. She grew up in Sweden and came to the UK to study at Edinburgh University in 2005. Her research interests centre on romantic and modern literary theory.

NICHOLA SMALLEY is a PhD student researching the translation of contemporary Swedish literature at UCL Department of Scandinavian Studies. She has worked as a translator for a few years, but this is her first attempt at professional literary translation.

ANNA TEBELIUS was born in Stockholm, educated in Paris and London and is currently pursuing a PhD degree at UCL, attempting to translate the experimental and intertextual writings of the Finland-Swedish author Willy Kyrklund and translating contemporary poetry and prose.

Some other books from Norvik Press

Juhani Aho: The Railroad (translated by Owen Witesman)
Kjell Askildsen: *A Sudden Liberating Thought* (translated by Sverre Lyngstad)
Victoria Benedictsson: *Money* (translated by Sarah Death)
Hjalmar Bergman: *Memoirs of a Dead Man* (translated by Neil Smith)
Jens Bjørneboe: *Moment of Freedom* (translated by Esther Greenleaf Mürer)
Jens Bjørneboe: *Powderhouse* (translated by Esther Greenleaf Mürer)
Jens Bjørneboe: *The Silence* (translated by Esther Greenleaf Mürer)
Johan Borgen: *The Scapegoat* (translated by Elizabeth Rokkan)
Kerstin Ekman: *Witches' Rings* (translated by Linda Schenck)
Kerstin Ekman: *The Spring* (translated by Linda Schenck)
Kerstin Ekman: *The Angel House* (translated by Sarah Death)
Kerstin Ekman: *City of Light* (translated by Linda Schenck)
Arne Garborg: *Tha Making of Daniel Braut* (translated by Marie Wells)
Svava Jakobsdóttir, *Gunnlöth's Tale* (translated by Oliver Watts)
P. C. Jersild: *A Living Soul* (translated by Rika Lesser)
Selma Lagerlöf: *Lord Arne's Silver* (translated by Sarah Death)
Selma Lagerlöf: *The Löwensköld Ring* (translated by Linda Schenck)
Selma Lagerlöf: *The Phantom Carriage* (translated by Peter Graves)
Viivi Luik: *The Beauty of History* (translated by Hildi Hawkins)
Henry Parland: *To Pieces* (translated by Dinah Cannell)
Amalie Skram: *Lucie* (translated by Katherine Hanson and Judith Messick)
Amalie and Erik Skram: *Caught in the Enchanter's Net: Selected Letters* (edited and translated by Janet Garton)
August Strindberg: *Tschandala* (translated by Peter Graves)
August Strindberg: *The Red Room* (translated by Peter Graves)
Hjalmar Söderberg: *Martin Birck's Youth* (translated by Tom Ellett)
Hjalmar Söderberg: *Selected Stories* (translated by Carl Lofmark)
Anton Tammsaare: *The Misadventures of the New Satan* (translated by Olga Shartze and Christopher Moseley)
Elin Wägner: *Penwoman* (translated by Sarah Death)

August Strindberg's One-Act Plays: A Selection

by

August Strindberg

Translated from the Swedish
by Agnes Broomé, Anna Holmwood,
John K Mitchinson, Mathelinda Nabugodi,
Anna Tebelius and Nichola Smalley

Norvik Press
2012

Originally published in Swedish by Johan Grönstedt under the title *Den Fredlöse – Nu – månadsskrift* (1876), and by Albert Bonniers förlag under the following titles: *Bandet – Tryckt och otryckt, ny samling* (1897); *Inför döden – Dramatik* (1893); *Samum – Tryckt och otryckt I* (1890).

This translation, translators' notes and introduction © Agnes Broomé, Anna Holmwood, John K Mitchinson, Mathelinda Nabugodi, Anna Tebelius and Nichola Smalley 2012.

The translator's moral right to be identified as the translator of the work has been asserted.

Norvik Press Series B: English Translations of Scandinavian Literature, no. 55

A catalogue record for this book is available from the British Library.

ISBN: 978-1-870041-93-5

Norvik Press gratefully acknowledges the generous support of Kulturrådet (Swedish Arts Council) towards the publication of this translation.

Norvik Press
Department of Scandinavian Studies
University College London
Gower Street
London WC1E 6BT
United Kingdom
Website: www.norvikpress.com
E-mail address: norvik.press@ucl.ac.uk
Managing editors: Sarah Death, Helena Forsås-Scott, Janet Garton, C. Claire Thomson.

Cover illustration: *Celestograph XIII* (1893-94) by August Strindberg, National Library of Sweden, Collection of Manuscripts, Strindbergsrummet.

Layout: Elettra Carbone
Cover design: Elettra Carbone
Printed in the UK by Lightning Source UK Ltd.

Contents

Foreword 9

The Outlaw 13
Translators' note 44

Simoom 49
Translators' note 62

Facing Death 65
Translators' note 84

The Bond 87
Translators' note 122

*Ve människorna ... änglar äro de icke;
men det är synd om dem.*
August Strindberg

Foreword

August Strindberg was and remains one of Sweden's most versatile artists; a dedicated painter, musician, photographer and journalist, he is nevertheless most famous for his literary works and in particular his drama. Plays such as *Miss Julie* and *The Father*, which helped establish Naturalism as a dramatic movement, have been translated into a range of languages and are still two of the most frequently performed Scandinavian plays worldwide. The following collection presents four less well-known one act plays which together begin to reveal to the reader a different Strindberg, who transcends the Naturalism with which he has become so intimately associated; a dramatist whose temperament called for ceaseless innovation and whose talents assured his success across a remarkable range of genres.

The four plays in this volume span the first half of Strindberg's career and reflect many of the trends evident in his wider production. *The Outlaw*, written in 1871, is a historical drama, as were most of Strindberg's early plays, inspired by his reading of ancient Icelandic literature while at university and notable for its not entirely successful attempt to recreate the terse language of the sagas. In Simoom, a practically gothic piece written as early as 1889 and inspired by Edgar Allan Poe, we can already begin to see Strindberg's shift away from Naturalism toward the fantastical and experimental dream technique that he pioneered, which would reach its fullest expression in his *A Dream Play* over a decade later. *Facing*

Death and *The Bond*, both written in the prodigiously prolific year 1892, are two fine examples of Strindberg's own brand of Naturalism, which does not limit itself to detailed slice-of-life descriptions of the everyday. Instead, what Strindberg himself termed 'Great Naturalism' seeks out points of extreme conflict, the unusual, and aims to show 'a piece of nature through a temperament'. In *Facing Death* and *The Bond*, Strindberg's temperament is very clearly in evidence and his habit of drawing on personal experience for his dramatic material no less so. Both plays are dark depictions of marriage and family life, influenced by the gradual deterioration and final demise of Strindberg's first marriage. Taken together, the plays in this collection will allow the reader to traverse vast geographical and temporal space, from the bitter cold of Viking age Iceland to the scorching desserts of colonised Algeria, meeting along the way Strindberg in his many varied guises.

Some of the more exotic features of these plays can make them feel eccentric and unfamiliar, but readers will also find much that unites them and sets them in clear relation to Strindberg's wider production. Most prominently, all four are based on the premise of a conflict between opposing and irreconcilable forces; in *The Outlaw* the central conflict is between Paganism and Christianity, in *Simoom* between coloniser and colonised and in *The Bond* between divorcing spouses. More importantly, beneath these obvious surface tensions, there is in all four plays a dark undertow of more primal conflict, a 'clash of natural forces', between parents and children, men and women, progress and tradition. This is where Strindberg is truly in his element and he spares neither his reader nor his own characters in his search for what he himself called 'the points where the great battles are fought'. Each play in this volume is a superb example of the psychological drama that was Strindberg's greatest strength. The worlds created in the plays are all, though superficially so very different, passionate, claustrophobic spaces in which human relationships are exaggerated to terrifying intensity. The reader can only watch as Strindberg mercilessly pits the members of the casts against each other in situations where love has turned into the ultimate weapon and where death and destruction is the only possible outcome.

*

August Strindberg is without a doubt Sweden's most famous and fascinating playwright, but today, one hundred years after his passing, many of his works are frequently overlooked or even entirely forgotten. In this year when the world celebrates the centenary of the great man's death, what could be more appropriate than publishing new translations of some of the plays that have long been unavailable to readers in the UK? The four translations in this book are the products of a mentorship programme generously supported by University College London and the Swedish Arts Council. The programme has given six emerging literary translators, grouped into three pairs, the opportunity to work closely with an experienced mentor in a profoundly collaborative process aimed at developing their skills and art. We all hope that you will enjoy this book and meet in it the infuriating, compelling and profound Strindberg that greeted us in the originals.

Agnes Broomé

The Outlaw

(1871)

Translated from the Swedish
by Anna Holmwood and John K Mitchinson

CAST

THORFINN
VALGERD
GUNLÖD
GUNNAR
ORM
Minor characters.

In Iceland in about 1100.

A small house. Door in the background. Unglazed windows are closed with wooden shutters. Wall-mounted benches, with the High Seat stage left. The pillars of the High Seat are carved with images of Odin and Thor. A lit hearth centre stage, a smoke hole above it. Viking swords, axes and shields hang on the wall beams.

The Outlaw

GUNLÖD *(stands by the open window looking out. Through this the sea is visible, illuminated by the northern lights)*. VALGERD *(sits by the hearth, spinning)*.

VALGERD: Close the window!
GUNLÖD *(is silent.)*
VALGERD: Gunlöd!
GUNLÖD: You spoke, mother?
VALGERD: What are you doing?
GUNLÖD: I'm looking at the sea.
VALGERD: When will you learn to let go?
GUNLÖD: Take everything from me, but let me keep the memory!
VALGERD: Look ahead or you'll fall!
GUNLÖD: Who begrudges the strong Viking a look back as he leaves his shore?
VALGERD: You've had three winters to say goodbye.
GUNLÖD: You're right, three winters, for summer never made it here.
VALGERD: When the ice melts it will be spring!
GUNLÖD: The northern lights can't melt ice!
VALGERD: Neither can your tears.
GUNLÖD: You've never seen me cry.
VALGERD: I've heard it, and until you stop, you'll remain a child.
GUNLÖD: I'm not a child.
VALGERD: If you want to be a woman, suffer, but suffer in silence.
GUNLÖD: I'll banish the grief from my mind, mother.
VALGERD: No, no! Hide it like your most precious possession. The seed must lie in the ground if it's to produce grain. Your grief is profound and it will bring great peace and great joy.
GUNLÖD *(after a pause)*: I will forget.
VALGERD: Everything?
GUNLÖD: I'll try!
VALGERD: Are you going to forget your father's harshness?
GUNLÖD: I have forgotten it!
VALGERD: Do you want to forget your ancestral home that

stood on the shores of Bråviken in the Kingdom of the Svear, the southern wind that sung among the oaks as the ice broke and the scent of the spruce and the chirping of the finches in the linden trees and the way the camomile rocked you to sleep on green meadows – do you want to forget all this, now that you hear lamenting gulls on bare rocks and the northern snowstorms howling through stunted birches?

GUNLÖD: Yes!

VALGERD: Do you want to forget that you had a childhood friend from whom your father tore you away to save you from the white Christ?

GUNLÖD *(with despair)*: Yes! Yes!

VALGERD: Now you're crying.

GUNLÖD *(worried)*: There's someone on the porch. Maybe father has come home!

VALGERD: Do you want to be reminded every day, without tears, that we live in the land of eternal ice, refugees from the Kingdom of the Svear and even though we don't perform sacrifices, we are threatened by the Christians because we refuse to be baptised and kiss the bishop's hand. Have you spoken to any of the Christians since we came here?

GUNLÖD *(after a pause)*: No! - - - Mother, is it true that father is to become an earl in Iceland?

VALGERD: Don't let that worry you, child!

GUNLÖD: Oh! Then I fear that he will treat the Christians badly.

VALGERD: You fear it?

GUNLÖD: There's someone outside.

VALGERD *(worried)*: Did you see the ship in the fjord this morning?

GUNLÖD: Oh yes! What a rare pleasure!

VALGERD: Did she bear the emblem of Thorfinn?

GUNLÖD: I couldn't make it out.

VALGERD: Be careful, girl!

GUNLÖD: Is it this evening that I am allowed to go out?

VALGERD: Tomorrow, and you know it.

GUNLÖD: Mother!

VALGERD *(as she leaves)*: Look after the fire.

GUNLÖD *(watches her mother leave, before carefully taking out a cross carved with the figure of Christ, placing it on the High Seat and falling to her knees.)*: Christ! Christ! Forgive me the lie I told. *(Jumps up when she sees the pictures on the pillars on the High Seat.)* No, I cannot pray with the wicked pictures watching me. *(She looks for another place.)* Holy Saint George and Holy - - - oh, how could I forget what the Bishop called her – God! God! – Don't throw me into purgatory for this sin – I will recite the whole long and difficult prayer in the language of the monks – credo – credo – in patrem – oh, I've forgotten that too – I'll burn five large wax candles at the altar of God's mother the next time I go to chapel – credo in patrem omnipotentem – *(Kisses the cross ardently.)*
(Singing outside, accompanied by lyre.)

> A crusader set out for eastern lands,
> To pray there for his long-lost love,
> O Christ, take my fair maiden's soul in Thy hands,
> Let her into Thy Kingdom above! –
> I will return when the linden she blooms.
>
> For two summers out there did he remain,
> Where the nightingale sings in the eve,
> And mass he did hold in the night and the day
> In the chapel of the holy grave –
> I will return when the linden she blooms.
>
> When the palms bud there on fair Jordan's shore,
> He prays to his God in that place,
> To be able to return homewards once more
> And feel his fair bride's warm embrace.
> I will return when the linden she blooms!

GUNLÖD *(who jumped up at the start of the song to listen to it, goes to the door once it has finished and goes to bolt it, but does this so slowly that Gunnar is able to slip through.)*
GUNNAR *(enters, dressed as a crusader, with a lyre on his*

shoulder.)
(They embrace.)
GUNLÖD *(pulls away and goes towards the door.)*
GUNNAR: You're afraid of me – what is it, Gunlöd?
GUNLÖD: You never held me like that before.
GUNNAR: We were children then!
GUNLÖD: You're right – we were children then. *(Pause.)* What does that silver falcon on your shield mean? I saw it this morning on your ship.
GUNNAR: You saw my ship, you recognised my song and still you wanted to close the door to me; how am I to understand you, Gunlöd?
GUNLÖD: Oh, don't ask me anything, I'm in such a strange mood; but sit down and let me speak to you.
GUNNAR *(sits.)*
(Pause.)
GUNNAR *(pulls her into his arms.)*

Gunlöd! Gunlöd! Has the snow fallen so heavily that your memory has frozen? Even the glacier out there can cry tears of fire, yet you are as cold as a snowstorm; but speak – speak! – Why are you here? What's happened?

GUNLÖD: Bad things have happened, and worse will happen if you stay longer – *(Jumps up.)* Go, before my father comes!
GUNNAR: Do you think I'd let you go now – I who have searched for you for so many years? When I couldn't find you in our land, I went to fight Saracens and black men to find you beyond the grave, but my time was not yet come and as the fourth spring came round, I heard that you were here. Now I have you and you want me to leave you alone in this heathen darkness!
GUNLÖD: I'm not alone!
GUNNAR: Your father doesn't love you – your mother doesn't understand you and both are heathens.
GUNLÖD: I have Christian friends!
GUNNAR: Then you are a Christian, Gunlöd! The Holy Virgin heard my prayer.
GUNLÖD: Yes! Yes! Oh, let me kiss the cross you bear on your

shoulder. You must have received it from the Holy Grave?

GUNNAR: And now I give you our Christian brethren's kiss, the first you have received from me, Gunlöd.

GUNLÖD: You must never kiss me again!

GUNNAR: But, tell me, how did you become a Christian?

GUNLÖD: First I believed in my father – he was so strong; then I believed in my mother – she was so good; until finally I believed in you – you were so strong and so good and – so handsome; and when you left I was alone – I could never believe in myself, because I was so weak. Then I remembered your God, the one you so often bade me love – and I prayed to him.

GUNNAR: And the old gods?

GUNLÖD: I have never been able to believe in them, although father commanded me to – they are so wicked.

GUNNAR: And who taught you to confess and gave you this image of Christ?

GUNLÖD: The Bishop.

GUNNAR: And no-one knows?

GUNLÖD: No, no-one, because I have had to hide it from my mother, and it worries me so.

GUNNAR: And your father hid you here, so that the Christians wouldn't find you?

GUNLÖD: Yes, and now he's on his way from Norway, where he has gathered men. He wishes to be an earl on the island!

GUNNAR: God forbid!

GUNLÖD: Yes – yes – but you mustn't stay longer because he's expected home this evening.

GUNNAR: Well then, beyond the headland at Hjörleifsnäset is my boat; let's out to sea! There is an offshore wind, and we will be in Orkney before the first cock crows.

GUNLÖD: Oh yes!

GUNNAR: Soon we will be back in Östergötland; there it is still summer and still green, and you will live in my castle, which I built where your father's farm once stood!

GUNLÖD: It's gone?

GUNNAR: Yes, it was burned down.

GUNLÖD: By the Christians?

GUNNAR: You are so quick tempered, Gunlöd.

GUNLÖD: I wish I were a heathen.

GUNNAR: What are you saying, girl?

GUNLÖD: Forgive me! Forgive me! – I have such a wild temper – and when I see pious Christians acting like –

GUNNAR: Kill that thought, it's godless. Do you see this wreath?

GUNLÖD: Where did you get it?

GUNNAR: You know these flowers, Gunlöd?

GUNLÖD: They grew in my father's herb garden; may I have them?

GUNNAR: Of course – but what do you need them for when we are about to leave?

GUNLÖD: I will look at them when the long winter comes: the spruce will remind me of the green forest and the forget-me-nots of the blue skies.

GUNNAR: But they are already withered.

GUNLÖD: I didn't think of that!

GUNNAR: Then come with me from this dreadful island back to where our childhood was spent, we can live as free as birds among flowers, sunshine and warmth! You will never again need to sneak to the Lord's temple when the Sabbath bells ring. Oh, you shall see the new church with the arched roof and the high cloisters and hear the song of the deacons when the Bishop lights the frankincense by the high altar. There you shall celebrate mass with the Christians – and you will see how your heart forgets everything!

GUNLÖD: Am I to flee from my mother?

GUNNAR: She'll forgive you one day.

GUNLÖD: But my father will call me a coward. I won't allow it.

GUNNAR: You must suffer that for the sake of your faith.

GUNLÖD: Thorfinn's daughter was never a coward.

GUNNAR: Your father doesn't love you and he will hate you when he learns of your conversion.

GUNLÖD: That he may – but he'll never despise me.

GUNNAR: Now you're being a coward, Gunlöd!

GUNLÖD: No! Isn't it greater to bear his hate than to flee his contempt?

GUNNAR: You compromise your love, Gunlöd!

GUNLÖD: Love?! - - - I remember my wet-nurse telling me about a young maiden. A friend left her and she was never happy again. She sat there, sewing in silk and gold. No one was allowed to see what it was she was sewing, and when they asked she cried, and when they asked why she was crying she wouldn't answer but kept sobbing. Her cheeks grew pale and her mother prepared the shroud. Then an old woman came and said that – it was love. Gunnar, I never cried when you left because father says that crying brings shame, I never sewed silk and gold, for my mother never taught me. Was I not in love?

GUNNAR: Have you often thought about me during these long years?

GUNLÖD: I have dreamed of you so very often, and when this morning I stood by the window, where I so love to stand looking out at the sea, and saw your ship appear in the east I felt anxious; I didn't know it was yours, of course.

GUNNAR: And why do you enjoy looking out to sea so much?

GUNLÖD: So many questions!

GUNNAR: Why did you want to close the door to me?

GUNLÖD *(is silent.)*

GUNNAR: Why didn't you close it?

GUNLÖD *(is silent.)*

GUNNAR: Why won't you say anything?

GUNLÖD *(bursts into heavy sobs.)*

GUNNAR: You're crying, Gunlöd, and you don't know why! I know why – you're in love. *(Takes her in his arms and kisses her.)*

GUNLÖD *(pulls away)*: You are not to kiss me – go!

GUNNAR: Yes – and you will come with me.

GUNLÖD: I don't take orders from you. I won't obey you.

GUNNAR: The glacier spits fire – and puts itself out.

GUNLÖD: You have disturbed my peace – for ever – go and let me forget you!

GUNNAR: Do you want to know what the silver falcon with the

ribbon means? It's the wild girl I will tame.

GUNLÖD: You! – Go, before I start to hate you! – No-one has tamed me yet!

GUNNAR: Wild blood – still simmering with Viking fire – but it will go out! Gunlöd – I will wait for one day – and you shall come – mild as a dove seeking shelter, even if now you're a falcon wanting to fly above the clouds. I still hold the band – it is your love – and it is a bond that can't be broken. When the light fades tomorrow you will come – Until then, farewell! *(Goes to the door, where he stops.)*

GUNLÖD *(is silent.)*

GUNNAR: Farewell!

GUNLÖD: We will see, o proud crusader, who comes first. I will come when this wreath next turns to green. *(Throws the wreath on the fire. She stands deep in thought as it burns. Once it has burned up, she bursts into tears and falls to her knees.)* God! God! Bend my hard will – otherwise I will never be your child – oh, that he would go! (Hurries to the door – at that moment Valgerd enters and walks past Gunlöd to the fire.)

VALGERD: Why haven't you looked after the fire?

GUNLÖD *(is silent.)*

VALGERD *(places her hand on Gunlöd's heart)*: You're keeping something secret.

GUNLÖD: Yes, mother, yes!

VALGERD: Hide it well!

GUNLÖD: No, I must speak – I can no longer –

VALGERD: When did you see a mother who didn't know her daughter's secrets?

GUNLÖD: Who has told you mine?

VALGERD *(harshly)*: Dry your tears!

(Pause.)

GUNLÖD: Oh, let me go outside to the mountains or the shore – it's stifling in here!

VALGERD: Go upstairs, you will be alone there!

A THRALL *(enters.)*

VALGERD: What do you want?

THRALL: The Earl's horns can be heard beyond the rocks and

the storm is growing!

VALGERD: Has night fallen?

THRALL: Yes, and the darkness is terrible!

(Pause.)

GUNLÖD: Send out a boat – or two – as many as can be found.

THRALL: All the boats are out hunting!

GUNLÖD: Light the beacons!

THRALL: The wood is so wet we haven't been able to kindle a fire all evening.

VALGERD: Go!

THRALL: What will become of the Earl?

VALGERD: Does it concern you?

THE THRALL *(leaves.)*

GUNLÖD: Have you forgotten your anger?

VALGERD: No, nor my desire for revenge – no one lays a hand on the daughter of an Earl!

GUNLÖD: Well! The time is come. Take your revenge, here – I will teach you! *(Takes a torch.)* Put this torch in the right-hand window, and you will break him; put it in the left and you will make him…

VALGERD: Give me the stick and be gone!

GUNLÖD: There is one sacrifice that will appease your gods – sacrifice your revenge! *(Leaves.)*

VALGERD *(takes the torch and quickly goes over to the left-hand window which she then opens. Horns can be heard outside)*: You struck me, Thorfinn. I swear I will have my revenge. I will humiliate you with my kindness at least.

GUNLÖD *(who has entered unnoticed by Valgerd, puts her arms around her mother's neck)*: Thank you, mother!

VALGERD *(embarrassed)*: Haven't you gone…?

GUNLÖD: Now I can go… *(Leaves.)*

VALGERD *(alone by the window)*: You call for help, strong man, you who always helped yourself. *(The sound of horns.)* Where is your power – where is your kingdom going? *(A gust of wind shakes the shutter and extinguishes the torch. Valgerd jumps up, terrified, and lights the torch again.)* Oh! – he is dying. What am I to do! – Pray! To whom? – Odin? Njord?

Agir? – I have called upon them now for two score years, but they have never answered! I have offered sacrifices to them, but they have never helped. You, God, whatever your name is – you, the mighty one, who causes the sun to rise and set, you, the powerful one, who commands the winds and the waters, to you I will pray. I will sacrifice my revenge to you if you save him!

ORM *(enters unseen)*: Good evening, Lady Valgerd! Put on your cloak, the air is biting!

VALGERD *(embarrassed, closes the shutter and takes down the torch)*: Welcome, Orm!

ORM: Thank you, lady.

VALGERD: How are you Orm?

ORM: Well enough, when I'm by the fire.

VALGERD *(impatient)*: How was the journey, I mean?

ORM: That's a long story.

VALGERD: Make it short!

ORM: Well, as you know, we were to travel to Norway to find men and timber!

VALGERD: Orm!

ORM: Lady Valgerd!

VALGERD: You haven't said a word about the Earl.

ORM: Did you ask after your husband?

VALGERD: Where is he? Is he alive?

ORM: I don't know!

VALGERD: You don't know? You, his foster brother? Where were you separated?

ORM: Oh, far out in the fjord. It was a funny sight, believe me. You should have seen him, swimming with my lyre in his hand. He promised to look after it; the seaweed was caught up in his hair and beard, he looked like the water spirit himself. At that moment a wave, as big as a house came –

VALGERD: And then... ?

ORM: Then – I never saw my lyre again!

VALGERD: Orm! You make jokes when your master and brother may be perishing out there. I command you, go at once and find him. Do you hear me!

ORM: What's happened to you? You never used to ask about your husband. You could at least give me some beer before I go!

VALGERD: Warm your knees by the stove. I am going – I will fight wave and storm!

ORM *(takes her hands)*: Woman! Woman! – You're only a woman!

VALGERD *(angry)*: Let go of my hand!

ORM: Now the Earl is saved!

VALGERD: Saved!

ORM: Yes, he has got you back again – and that is just what he needs now! *(Leaves.)*

(Thorfinn and Orm can be heard outside. Thorfinn laughs loudly.)

VALGERD: The Earl is coming – he is laughing, I've never heard that before. Oh, something terrible is brewing!

THORFINN and ORM *(enter.)*

THORFINN *(laughing)*: That was a funny sight.

ORM: Yes, it certainly was!

VALGERD: Welcome home, husband!

THORFINN: Thank you, wife! Have you been out in the rain? Your eyes are wet!

VALGERD: You are so amusing –

THORFINN: Amusing – yes! Yes!

VALGERD: What became of your ships?

ORM: They went to the bottom, all but one.

VALGERD *(to Thorfinn)*: And yet you're happy.

THORFINN: Ha! A lot of wood grows on the northern slopes!

ORM: Now perhaps it's time to get something to eat!

THORFINN: Well said! Wife, get the beer so we may enjoy ourselves.

ORM: And thank the gods for saving us.

THORFINN: When will you grow out of those stories, Orm!

ORM: Why do you force your daughter and wife to believe in them?

THORFINN: Womenfolk need gods.

ORM: Who do you think helped out there?

THORFINN: I did it myself!

ORM: And still you screamed to Thor the Charioteer when the

big wave swallowed you!

THORFINN: Liar!

ORM: Orm never lies!

THORFINN: Orm is a poet!

ORM: Thorfinn must have swallowed too much sea water when he called for help – because his mouth is so salty!

THORFINN: Control your tongue, Orm!

VALGERD *(with a horn)*: Here we are, brothers! I drink to your friendship and better fortune for your next voyage!

THORFINN: I forbid you to speak more of this!

(They drink.)

THORFINN *(takes the horn from his mouth and asks)*: Where is the child?

VALGERD *(worried)*: She is upstairs.

THORFINN: Call her here!

VALGERD: She is sick!

THORFINN *(glares at Valgerd)*: She will come!

VALGERD: You don't want that!

THORFINN: Did you hear my command?

VALGERD: Not for the last time.

THORFINN: A man is as good as his word, yet his woman must always have the last word!

VALGERD *(weakly)*: You mock me.

THORFINN: I think you're angry.

VALGERD: You laugh so much this evening! *(Leaves.)*

THORFINN: Orm! I've had a thought!

ORM: If it's big, then hide it. Big ideas are hard to come by!

THORFINN: Did you see my wife?

ORM: I never look at other men's wives.

THORFINN: How friendly and pleasant she was.

ORM: She felt sorry for you!

THORFINN: Sorry for me?

ORM: Yes, because laughing sorrows are lethal sorrows – she thought!

THORFINN: A woman cannot think!

ORM: No! – Not with her head, but with her heart; therefore she has a smaller head, but bigger breasts than us!

THORFINN: Evil feelings torment me!

ORM: Poor Thorfinn!

THORFINN: My child! ... Orm! When she comes, you are to invite her to drink from the horn of Odin.

ORM: The fox is sniffing the wind – I understand!

THORFINN: Be ready – they're coming.

ORM: If you are hard on the child, Thorfinn, you'll have me to deal with!

VALGERD and GUNLÖD *(enter. The latter looks sleepy.)*

GUNLÖD: Welcome home, father!

THORFINN: Is it true?

GUNLÖD *(is silent.)*

THORFINN: Are you sick?

GUNLÖD: I don't feel particularly well!

THORFINN: So I fear!

ORM: Gunlöd, now you shall empty the blessed horn to Odin, who saved your father from disaster at sea.

(Takes the horn, holds it over the fire and passes it to Gunlöd. All empty their horns but Gunlöd.)

THORFINN *(trembling)*: Drink, Gunlöd!

GUNLÖD *(throws the horn to the floor – goes forward and lays her head on Thorfinn's lap)*: Listen, father: I am a Christian. Do what you want with me, but you can't destroy my soul – God and the saints will protect it!

THORFINN *(stands up, wild with pain and anger, pushes Gunlöd aside and tries to speak. Words fail him. He sits down on the bench in silence.)*

ORM *(goes to the women and speaks slowly to them. They go towards the door, at which point Gunlöd runs back and stands opposite Thorfinn.)*

GUNLÖD: No! I will not go. I must speak, so that you, my father, will not go to the grave with a lie. Your whole life has been one! I will sacrifice childish deference – for love I have never known – and show you what tremendous guilt you have hanging over you. No! You taught me to hate – for when did you give me love – you taught me to fear the great Earl Thorfinn and you succeeded. I tremble before your harshness and I respect your many years and your great deeds. But you never taught me to love my father! You pushed me away every time I wanted to get close to you. You poisoned my soul, but now you see God's punishment. – You have made me an outcast – because that's what I am at this moment, but I can do nothing else. Why do you hate my faith? It must be because it's love and yours is hate! – Oh father! Father! I wanted to comfort you in your old age, I wanted to kiss the clouds from your brow, I wanted to stroke your white hair and make you forget the sorrows that whitened it. I wanted to support you when your steps began to falter. Oh! Forget what I have said and open your heart (*on her knees*) and lift me up – look at me tenderly just once before it's too late. Say something ... (*Jumps up.*) – Oh, your look is so cold, it's killing me! – You won't? – I will pray for the strength to damn you! (*Bursts into tears and leaves, followed by Valgerd.*)

ORM (*goes over to Thorfinn.*)

THORFINN: Sing, Orm!

ORM: Orm sings only lies!

THORFINN: Then lie!

ORM: Is the truth so bitter?

THORFINN: What are you saying!

ORM: Oh yes, you will hear more from me later. Now I will calm the beast with a beautiful untruth! (*Takes his harp and performs the following ballad with strokes of the lyre between each verse.*)

As spring wind passed
Over rocking seas
And shoots broke through
brown earth,
Then the King drew
his boat from its berth,
To try to journey
On foaming wave.

We set the rudder

The Outlaw

For Leiregård
There we drank mead
With the King of the Danes.
Then on eastwards
To Micklegård's chambers,
Where we enjoyed grapes
With the dark-eyed maiden.

Shields were raised
To high mast,
Chain mail cracked
And shields smashed.
The arrows sang
'It is spring', 'It is spring'
Like sap from birches
Blood ran from wounds.

No woman dared
Refuse our embrace.
And from the farmer at his plough
We took what we could.
Yet defiantly he hid
His goods and his gold,
So we roasted his cattle
Over flames in his yard.

How glorious, glorious,
Life was then!
As rolling waves tightened
Around iron-clad posts,
Viking hearts beat,
With a lust for life
And riotous ballads
Sang out from our harps.
In poets' ballads
Word of Norse strength
Was sung across

Our wide world.
Now the sword rusts
And weakness is worshipped,
While the Sea-King sleeps
By a sooty hearth.

What's a poet to sing
In times without mighty deeds?
Steel strings are not
For babble and show.
I will hang my harp,
Hang it on the wall,
As I sing farewell
To great deeds and power.

THORFINN *(waking from his thoughts)*: Is it over?
ORM: Yes, that's usually the end of the song.
THORFINN: Orm, you are my friend!
ORM: Hmm – that's right!
THORFINN: I miss peace and quiet.
ORM: There are two ways of finding peace: the first is never to do what you will regret; the second is never to regret what you do!
THORFINN: And if one has already done what one regrets?
ORM: Thorfinn! Then you regret your harshness towards the child?
THORFINN *(firmly)*: I never regret anything, and as far as the child is concerned –
ORM: Listen, Thorfinn, have you never thought about your past?
THORFINN: Thinking is what old women do by the fire. My life has been about doing!
ORM: What are you going to do now?
THORFINN: What am I going to do now?
ORM: Yes!
THORFINN *(hurt, is silent.)*
ORM: See how that little thought hit you; imagine if it had

been a great one. - - - Why are you so scared to look back? It's because you fear you will see a terrible sight!

THORFINN: And what about letting the past be buried?

ORM: No! I will tear up the dead from their mounds and they will stare at you with empty eyes, until you collapse and tremble in fear – and then you will see that you, even with all your power, never were a man!

THORFINN: What are you talking about, you madman?

ORM: Scream if you want: You're still just a boy, yes, you. I've seen big, tall boys with thick beards, grey hair and crooked spines.

THORFINN: Hold your tongue, Orm!

ORM: Scream till the house falls – you'll never drown out the truth.

THORFINN: Silence, before I hit you!

ORM: Hit me; beat me to death, pull the tongue from my mouth. The truth will still resound through copper horns and into your ears; "Your life was a lie!"

THORFINN *(suppressing anger and pain)*: Orm, I beg you – speak no more!

ORM: No, Thorfinn, I will speak! Do you feel how the ground is shaking beneath you? It's an earthquake! The whole world is shaking, because she will soon give birth. She will give birth to a hero under terrible pains. Open your eyes and see! Do you see how the peoples of the East and West are fighting each other? But soon the wedding will take place, and torches will be lit in their thousands and the whole earth will glow in peace and joy, for he will be born, the new, strong, beautiful King, who will rule over all peoples. He, whose sceptre is love and whose crown is light, and whose name is the new time! Not Christ, not the Pope. Thorfinn, do you remember the story of Thor competing against Utgårda Loki, Lord of the Giants? He lifted the cat so high that the troll turned pale, he drank so deep from the horn that the troll trembled, but when the old woman brought him to his knees, the troll laughed! Time conquered him and it is time that you are fighting and that has beaten you. The god that has crushed you is the Lord of Time!

THORFINN: I have never known any God other than my own power, and that is the one I believe in!

ORM: You don't know him; you, who have been fighting him for so long. It was he who drove you from the land of your forefathers and you thought you could escape him. It was he who smashed your ships to pieces and drowned your kingdom. All your power is gone. It was he who tore your child from you, and you say you miss peace and quiet. He was the one.

A MESSENGER *(enters)*: Are you Earl Thorfinn?

THORFINN: I am.

MESSENGER: You descended upon Reydafjord last spring!

THORFINN: I did!

MESSENGER: There you plundered and set fire to Hallfred's farm at Thorvaller.

THORFINN: Yes!

MESSENGER And then you went on your way!

THORFINN *(is silent.)*

MESSENGER: The courts have declared you an outlaw and a criminal. Your farm will be burned and whosoever will may take your life. Your enemies are about, therefore flee while you have time. Flee tonight! *(Leaves; there is a pause.)*

ORM: Do you know who that was?

THORFINN: That you may well ask!

ORM: He brought a message from the old times!

THORFINN: Silence, tramp.

ORM: These times don't want violence! You wronged them and now they beat you.

THORFINN: Time has no power, therefore it worships weakness.

ORM: Thorfinn! When you came to the island, you swore peace. You have broken your oath, you have wronged your honour. Therefore you will die as an outcast!

THORFINN: You too call me an outcast!

ORM: Yes!

THORFINN: If you dare to break an oath, you dare to be called an outcast!

ORM *(is silent.)*
THORFINN: Wretch! You are the one who ties me when I want to fly. You wind like a snake around my legs – let me go!
ORM: I have sworn the foster brother's oath.
THORFINN: And I'm breaking it.
ORM: You can't!
THORFINN: Then I will kick you away!
ORM: It will be the death of us!
THORFINN: Are you a man, Orm?
ORM: I'm only a poet!
THORFINN: Then you are nothing!
ORM: *I* knew what I wanted, but could do nothing – you could do everything, but didn't know what you wanted!
THORFINN: Thank you for your song! Farewell!
ORM: Who will sing your death song?
THORFINN: The ravens!
ORM: Do you dare to die? Thorfinn?
THORFINN: I dare more than to die – I dare to be forgotten!
ORM: You were always stronger than me. Farewell! We will meet again! *(Leaves.)*
THORFINN *(alone)*: Alone. Alone! Alone! ...
(Pause.)

I remember it was autumn –
The equinox storm raged with force
Over England's seas. – My boat was crushed
And I was thrown, alone, upon a desolate islet!
Then it was still – Oh, such long days!
Only cloudless skies above me
And endless deep-blue seas around me!
No sound of living beings!
No gull woke me with its scream!
Not even a breeze to make light waves
Splash against the rocks –
It seemed as though I myself were dead.
I spoke loudly, I screamed,
But my voice scared me,

And the dryness bound my tongue.
Only the steady beating of my heart
Reminded me that I was alive!
But after listening to its sound a while,
Soon I heard it no longer.
Then, full of fear, I arose
And so it continued until I fainted.
When I finally awoke – I heard
A slow heart beat beside me
And breathing from a mouth that was not mine,
And courage grew again in my soul.
I looked about me
It was a seal, who sought to rest;
It looked at me with wet eyes
As if it felt sympathy for me.
Then I was alone no longer;
I stretched out my hand to stroke
Its tough body. – Then it fled
And I was even more alone.
Now again I stand on an islet –
What do I fear? Yes, loneliness!
What is this loneliness? –
It is me, myself! –

(shaken)

Who am I then, do I fear myself?
Am I not Earl Thorfinn, the strong,
Who crushed thousands of wills with his own?
Who never needed friendship or lovemaking,
But carried all his sorrows himself!
No! No! I am someone else!
And that is who Thorfinn the strong is afraid of,
Thorfinn the weak! –
Who stole my power? Who hit me?
Was it the sea? Did I not hit the sea
Thirty times and it hit me

Just once – but it was a lethal strike!
It was stronger then – it is a God!
But who hit the sea so that it became still,
When it had been raging? Who? Who? Who?
It was the strongest?
Who then is the strongest!
Oh answer, so that I may believe in you!
He doesn't answer! – Everything is so quiet!
Now I hear the heart's beat once more!
Oh, help! Help!

(Goes to the door, calls) Valgerd!

THRALL: You called, my lord!

THORFINN *(calms down)*: You heard wrong!

THRALL: May I go then, Master?

THORFINN *(places his hand on the thrall's shoulder)*: No, you are to stay with me a while. Light torches, many torches; it is so dark in here. And put wood on the hearth. I am freezing. –

THRALL *(after having placed wood on the fire and lit the torches on the walls)*: Was there anything else?

THORFINN: You will carry out some errands.

THRALL: Yes, Master!

THORFINN: How many men do we have?

THRALL: Ah, two score and ten, I believe.

THORFINN: Are you scared to die, thrall?

THRALL: I shouldn't be, not when I'm expecting to be blessed! *(Makes the sign of the cross.)*

THORFINN: What does that mean?

THRALL: The Bishop taught it to us!

THORFINN: I forgot that you are a Christian!

THRALL: Why did you take me into your service, you who are a heathen!

THORFINN: I wanted to show how little I care for the beliefs of others. We shall double the bars across the northern gate!

THRALL: Yes, master! But belief is stronger than a hundred bars –

THORFINN: Did I ask you? *(Pause.)* How did you become a Christian here on this island?

THRALL: Oh, it was much easier than one would think. They just poured water on us as the Bishop read from a large book; and then we each received a white shirt!

THORFINN: Go tell the strongest twelve to get their new axes – do you hear!

THRALL: Yes, Master! *(About to leave.)*

THORFINN: You are not to leave yet! …… *(Pause.)* Do you remember what it said in the large book?

THRALL: I don't recall much, but I remember that he spoke about two criminals, who were hung on the cross together with God's son. But only one got to heaven.

THORFINN: Did they also pour water onto him?

THRALL: No, the Bishop didn't say so!

THORFINN: Do you know whether we have any horses in the stable?

THRALL: They are almost certainly out grazing, I will check.

THORFINN: Stay! *(Pause.)* Could you die in peace tonight?

THRALL: Yes, as long as I had time to pray first. –

THORFINN: And then one gains peace?

THRALL: Oh yes, Master!

THORFINN *(stands up and takes a goblet)*: You will receive this if you pray for me.

THRALL: It's not enough!

THORFINN: Then you shall have ten; but if you say a word about this, I will kill you!

THRALL: I wouldn't matter if you gave me a hundred, you must pray yourself!

THORFINN: I can't, but I order you to!

THRALL: I will obey; But you will see that it doesn't help. – Jesus Christ, have mercy on this poor sinner, who begs for your grace!

THORFINN: That is a lie – I never beg for anything!

THRALL: See, it hasn't helped you!

THORFINN: Take down my armour and help me.

THE THRALL *(helps him)*: You keep moving – I can't fasten it!

THORFINN: You are a wretch!

THRALL: But your whole body is shaking.

THORFINN: You are lying!
VALGERD and GUNLÖD *(enter.)*
THRALL: May I leave now?
THORFINN: Go!
VALGERD *(walks forward)*: You called me!
THORFINN: That's not true!
VALGERD: Your enemies are about!
THORFINN: And?
VALGERD: Prepare yourself. I heard what happened!
THORFINN: Then it's best that you hide out in the porch!
MESSENGER *(enters)*: Earl Thorfinn – we are here! Will you give yourself up?
THORFINN *(is silent.)*
MESSENGER: No answer! Let your women go, we are going to set fire to the house.
THORFINN *(is silent.)*
MESSENGER: Your answer!
GUNLÖD *(who was standing by the door takes an axe from the wall)*: I will give you the answer! How badly Earl Thorfinn would have raised his daughter and how little would his wife love him if they were to fail him now. There is your answer! *(Throws the axe before his feet.)*
MESSENGER: There are more of you than I thought, Thorfinn. For the sake of your daughter, you will be allowed to die as if you had not been an outcast. Prepare yourself to fight out on the fields! *(Leaves.)*
THORFINN *(to Valgerd)*: Shame on you, cowardly, treacherous woman, who guarded my treasure so poorly. – You made my child my enemy!
GUNLÖD: Oh father! Am I really your enemy?
THORFINN: You are a Christian; but it's not too late. Will you renounce your white Christ?
GUNLÖD: Never – but I will follow you in death!
VALGERD: Thorfinn! You called me a coward! That I must suffer, but treacherous? There you did me wrong! If I have not loved you as warmly as the women of the south are said to love, then I have at least been true to you my whole life, and

I have vowed to follow you. That is the old way. Look, I have prepared my grave – *(opens a hatch on the floor)* – here I will die, under these sooty beams that have been witness to my sorrow. I want to go up in flames together with these high benches that showed us the way here, and with the smoke, my spirit will rise up to Gimle!

GUNLÖD: Am I then to be on my own? Oh, let me follow you!

VALGERD: No, child, you are young, you can still be planted again under a milder sun; but the old pine dies where it stands!

GUNLÖD: Father! Father! You can't die! I will save you!

THORFINN: You?

GUNLÖD: Your kinsman Gunnar is beyond the headland at Hjörleifsnäset with his men; send a thrall to him by hidden way and he will come!

THORFINN: It was from there that you drew your courage. Keep your help and go if you want!

GUNLÖD: You mustn't call me a coward; I will follow you, mother; you can't stop me!

THORFINN *(goes to the door, hiding his emotion.)*

VALGERD: No, stay, Thorfinn, and open your soul for once so that I may decipher your runes!

THORFINN: Do you think I'll stand here explaining them? If you will not learn to understand them yourself let them be worn away as the stone erodes.

VALGERD: You are not the hard rock you seem; you have feelings – show them. Let them stream out. It will give you peace!

THORFINN: My feelings are the blood pumping in my heart – do you want to see that?

(The sounds of battle can be heard outside. This continues until Thorfinn comes back in. When Thorfinn hears it, he wants to leave.)

VALGERD: Oh, stay and say goodbye!

THORFINN: Woman, you break down my strength with your feelings. Let me go! The game has begun!

VALGERD: Oh say goodbye at least!

THORFINN *(leaves, making an effort to hide his emotion.)*
VALGERD: No one can bend that man.
GUNLÖD: God can!
VALGERD: He is so hard.
GUNLÖD: God's mercy is stronger!
VALGERD: Live well, my child!
GUNLÖD: Do you dare to leave me alone?
VALGERD *(embraces her)*: Are you ready?
GUNLÖD: The Holy Mother of God prays for me!
VALGERD: I put my hope in the God who is love.
GUNLÖD: And in the holy God's mother.
VALGERD: I don't know her.
GUNLÖD: You must believe in her!
VALGERD: Your belief is not mine!
GUNLÖD: Forgive me…
(They embrace.)
VALGERD: Take your place!
GUNLÖD *(opens the window and looks through.)*
VALGERD *(goes to the hole in the floor with a torch.)*
GUNLÖD: The fighting is fierce, mother!
VALGERD: Do you see the Earl?
GUNLÖD: He is standing in the entrance.
VALGERD: How does he seem?
GUNLÖD: All give way before him.
VALGERD: Is he tired?
GUNLÖD: He is still upright. Look at the northern lights!
VALGERD: Have many fallen?
GUNLÖD: I can't tell – they are drawing away from the yard. The sky is as red as blood!
(Pause.)
VALGERD: Speak – what do you see!
GUNLÖD *(delighted)*: The silver falcon!
VALGERD: What did you see?
GUNLÖD: I saw a falcon!
VALGERD: That means misfortune!
GUNLÖD: Father is coming!
VALGERD: Is he wounded?

GUNLÖD: Oh, he has fallen!

VALGERD: Close the door – it's in God's hands!

GUNLÖD: No, not yet – one moment!

VALGERD: Are you scared?

GUNLÖD: No! No! *(Goes towards the door. The noise from the battle slowly dies down.)*

THORFINN *(stumbles in, pale and wounded)*: Wait!

VALGERD *(goes towards him.)*

(Pause.)

THORFINN *(sits on the High Seat)*: Come here!

VALGERD and GUNLÖD *(go to him. He strokes Gunlöd's hair and kisses her forehead. He then takes Valgerd's hand.)*

THORFINN: Look, the blood pours from my heart now!

VALGERD *(stands up to take a torch)*: Now we have said our goodbye!

THORFINN: Stay… and live with your child!

VALGERD: My oath!

THORFINN: My whole life was a broken oath – and still I hope. It is greater to live ---

ORM *(enters, wounded, and stands by the door)*: May I come in?

THORFINN: Come!

ORM: Have you found peace now?

THORFINN: Soon! Soon! *(Caresses the women.)*

ORM: Are we ready to go?

THORFINN *(looks at Valgerd and Gunlöd)*: Not yet!

ORM *(sits on a bench)*: Hurry, if you want company?

THORFINN: Orm, are you a Christian?

ORM: That you may well ask!

THORFINN: What are you then… a mystery?

ORM: I was everything – I was nothing – I was a poet!

THORFINN: Do you believe in anything?

ORM: I found a faith.

THORFINN: Who gave it to you?

ORM: Doubt, sorrow!

THORFINN *(to Valgerd)*: Valgerd, give me your hand – there, there. Hold tight. Tighter. You mustn't let go until this is over!

GUNNAR *(enters, stands at the door.)*

THORFINN: Who's there?
GUNNAR: You know me!
THORFINN: I know your voice, but I can't see you!
GUNNAR: I am your kinsman, Gunnar!
(Pause.)
THORFINN: Come here!
GUNNAR *(stays where he is and gives Gunlöd a searching look.)*
THORFINN: Is he here?
GUNLÖD *(stands up and walks slowly, her head lowered, to Gunnar. She takes his hand and leads him to Thorfinn, where they both fall to their knees.)*
THORFINN *(places his hands on their heads):* God!
(Dies.)

Curtain

Translators' Note

Whether a translation can ever stand up to the timelessness accorded to an 'original' piece of literature is a question that will haunt any translation. This is especially pertinent for *The Outlaw* as we are not only translating it over one hundred and forty years after it was written, in 1871, but because it is itself an historical play. The layers of linguistic distance are therefore threefold; English to Swedish is only one dimension, there are the changes in the Swedish language itself since Strindberg was writing, in addition to choices Strindberg made to create his medieval historical setting, such as the inclusion of ballads. In translating this play in 2012, the question arose as to how we might tackle the overall tone of our translation. It would of course be beyond our expertise to translate Strindberg into 1871 English, and to do so would also misrepresent the linguistic distance we were experiencing. Strindberg was not deliberately making his language antiquated, so why should we?

Translations interact with literary and cultural references and the intricacies of word choice in the space between two languages as well as firmly within each. Strindberg had to teach himself to read in Old Norse the Icelandic sagas upon which this play was based, and through our translation the sagas must live again in another language, sagas as reworked by Strindberg as reworked by us. Strindberg makes use of different registers with *The Outlaw* and so too we had to find ways to give them expression. A medieval style ballad, a modern free verse monologue, to everyday speech refracted through the personalities and social standings of the different characters. Orm, Swedish for 'snake', speaks in playful tongue twisters, Gunnar preaches his stilted proclamations of love, Valgerd expresses angered passion, Gunlöd struggles to find her voice against the overbearing authority of her father and her lover, and Thorfinn pours forth in bombastic yet strangely hollow declarations. These are the beginnings of Strindberg's use of language as the staking out of (sexual) power.

That said, translating, like no other reading, puts an original text under an immense amount of scrutiny, and *The Outlaw* is not considered among Strindberg's best work. Written when he was still a student at the age of twenty-two, it does however foreshadow many themes which would go on to become important in his best known plays: the struggle for power between the sexes, faith versus reason, loyalty and betrayal. Yet there are elements to this play that upon first reading feel a little past their sell-by-date. The play draws upon notions of femininity as irrational, connected to the spiritual, and as changeable, threatening, disloyal. Thorfinn struggles to control the women of this play. But his obsession with loyalty reveals a wife and daughter more than capable of bravery and constancy, even when their independent thinking allows them to 'betray' Thorfinn's need to dominate. Ultimately Thorfinn's power is as empty of meaning as his belief in the old gods.

The Outlaw may not fundamentally challenge the association between female sexuality, irrationality and betrayal, but the play does continue to strike a chord with contemporary concerns, and it is perhaps here that the play will really find its new life. Women, their bodies and their sexuality, continue to be the sites for intense religious and secular debate. The lines between personal faith and political mobilisation are as fraught as ever, and embodied, sexually and politically active women are often viewed as the most potentially transgressive. *The Outlaw* is an historical play that still speaks to us. Our translation, however, has deliberately not pushed these associations to the fore, choosing instead to let these potential interpretations be read into the text rather be imposed by us through certain word choices. As with any play, the translation (and perhaps even the original text) is only the first and perhaps smallest step in giving it life again. A play lives on the stage, and it is here that the play, and our translation, should be judged.

Anna Holmwood and John K Mitchinson

Simoom

(1889)

Translated from the Swedish
by Nichola Smalley and Anna Tebelius

CAST

BISKRA, An Arabic girl, dressed as a male guide
YOUSSEF, her lover
GUIMARD, lieutenant in the French Zouave regiment, stationed in Algeria

Algeria.

An Arabic Marabout (tomb of a holy man), with a sarcophagus in the centre of the room. Prayer mats here and there; in the right hand corner a charnel house.
　In the background a door with hatches and fabric hangings; slit windows in the back wall. Small heaps of sand scattered around the floor; an uprooted aloe leaf, esparto grass in a pile.

Scene one

BISKRA. YOUSSEF.

BISKRA (*enters with a Burnous cape concealing her face and a guitar on her back, hurls herself down onto a mat and prays with her arms across her chest.*)
(*The wind howls outside.*)
BISKRA: La ilaha illa Allah
YOUSSEF (*rushes in*): Simoom is coming! Where's the Frenchman?
BISKRA: He'll be here any moment now!
YOUSSEF: Why didn't you cut him down at once?
BISKRA: No! He'll do it himself!
   If I did it they'd kill us all, because they know that I am Ali, the guide. But they don't know that I'm the girl, Biskra!
YOUSSEF: He'll do it himself? How will that work?
BISKRA: Don't you know, Simoom shrivels white men's brains like dried dates, giving them nightmarish visions that make their lives so loathsome they are driven headlong into the great unknown.
YOUSSEF: I've heard about this. At the last battle six Frenchmen had taken their own lives before they had even reached the battleground. But don't rely on Simoom today, for snow has fallen on the mountains and in half an hour the storm may have passed. – Biskra! Can you still hate?
BISKRA: Still hate? – My hatred is as boundless as the desert, it burns like the sun and is stronger than my love! Every moment of pleasure they have stolen from me since they killed Ali has gathered like venom in the fang of an asp, and what Simoom cannot do, I can.
YOUSSEF: Well spoken, Biskra, and you'll do it. Since I set eyes on you, my own hatred has withered like the desert grass in the autumn. Draw strength from me and be the arrow to my bow.
BISKRA: Embrace me, Youssef! Embrace me!

YOUSSEF: Not here in the presence of the Holy One; not now – later, afterwards! When you have earned your reward!

BISKRA: Proud Sheikh, proud man!

YOUSSEF: Yes – the girl who's going to carry my heir under her heart must prove herself worthy of the honour!

BISKRA: I alone shall carry Youssef's heir! I, Biskra – spurned, ugly, but strong!

YOUSSEF: Well! I'll go down and sleep by the spring! – Do I have to remind you of the mysterious arts you learnt from the great Holy Man Siddi-Sheikh, all the tricks you've practised at fairs since you were a child?

BISKRA: There's no need! – I have all the secret powers needed to frighten the wits out of a French coward; the coward, who sneaks up on his enemy and sends the bullet before him! I know everything – even the ventriloquist's art. And all that my arts cannot do, the sun shall do, as the sun is with Youssef and Biskra.

YOUSSEF: The sun is a Muslim's friend, but it can't be relied upon. You might burn yourself, girl! Take a drink of water, I see that your hands are shrivelling, and – *(He lifts a mat, and goes down for a bowl of water, which he hands to Biskra.)*

BISKRA *(raises the bowl to her mouth)*: – And my eye is beginning to see red – my lungs are drying out – I hear – I hear – look the sand is already pouring through the roof – and the strings of the guitar are singing – Simoom has arrived!! But the Frenchman has not!

YOUSSEF: Come down here, Biskra, and let the Frenchman die on his own!

BISKRA: First hell, then death! Do you think I'd break my promise! *(Empties the water on a pile of sand.)* I shall water the sand, then revenge will grow!

And I shall parch my heart. Hatred – grow! Sun – burn! Wind – smother!

YOUSSEF: Hail, mother of Ibn Youssef, it's you, you shall bear Youssef's son, the avenger!

(The wind intensifies; the fabric covering the door flaps; a red glow lights up the room, then during the following changes to

yellow.)
BISKRA: The Frenchman is coming, and – Simoom is here! – Go!
YOUSSEF: I'll return in half an hour! There's your hour-glass. *(Points to a heap of sand.)* The heavens will keep time for the infidel's hell!

Scene two

BISKRA. GUIMARD.

GUIMARD *(enters pale and unsteady, confused, speaks in a low voice)*: The Simoom is here! Where do you think my people went?
BISKRA: I led your people west to the East!
GUIMARD: West to the East! Let me see! It's right in the East and – the West! – Give me a seat, and water!
BISKRA *(leads Guimard to a heap of sand, places him on the ground with his head on the heap)*: Are you sitting comfortably?
GUIMARD *(gazes at her):* I'm sitting a little awkwardly. Put something under my head.
BISKRA *(piles the sand up under his head)*: There you are, a pillow for your head!
GUIMARD: My head? That's where my feet are! – Aren't my feet there?
BISKRA: Of course!
GUIMARD: I thought as much! – Give me a stool for my – head!
BISKRA *(drags the aloe and places it under Guimard's knees):* Here's your stool!
GUIMARD: And water! – Water!
BISKRA *(takes the empty bowl, fills it with sand and passes it to Guimard):* Drink it while it's cold!
GUIMARD *(sips from the bowl)*: It *is* cold – but it still isn't quenching my thirst – I can't drink water – I hate water – take it away!
BISKRA: There's the hound that bit you!
GUIMARD: What hound? No hound has ever bitten me.

BISKRA: The Simoom has darkened your memory – beware of its deceptions! Don't you remember the rabid hound that bit you at the next to last hunt in Bab-el-Oued.

GUIMARD: The hunt in Bab-el-Oued! That's right! Was it a beaver-coloured? –

BISKRA: – bitch? Yes! That's right! And he bit you in the calf! Can't you feel how the wound stings? –

GUIMARD *(touches his calf, and pricks himself on the aloe)*: Oh, yes I feel it! – Water! Water!

BISKRA *(passes him the bowl of sand)*: Drink, drink!

GUIMARD: No, I can't! Holy Mary, Mother of God – I've got rabies.

BISKRA: Don't be afraid; I'll heal you and drive out the demon with the almighty power of music! Listen!

GUIMARD *(shrieks)*: Ali! Ali! Not music! I can't bear it! And what use is it to me?

BISKRA: If the sly spirit of the serpent can be tamed by music, don't you think it can conquer the spirit of a raging hound! Listen! *(Sings as she strums the guitar.)* Biskra-Biskra, Biskra-Biskra, Biskra-Biskra, Simoom! Simoom!

YOUSSEF *(from below)*: Simoom! Simoom!

GUIMARD: What's that you're singing? Ali!

BISKRA: Was I singing? Look, I'll put a palm-leaf in my mouth! *(She puts a palm frond between her teeth. Song from above.)* Biskra-Biskra, Biskra-Biskra, Biskra-Biskra.

YOUSSEF *(from below)*: Simoom! Simoom!

GUIMARD: What sort of hellish farce is this?

BISKRA: Now I'm singing!

BISKRA and YOUSSEF *(together)*: Biskra-Biskra, Biskra-Biskra, Biskra-Biskra.

Simoom!

GUIMARD *(gets up)*: What kind of demon are you, singing with two tongues! Are you a man or a woman? Or both?

BISKRA: I am Ali, the guide! You don't recognise me because your senses are shrouded but if you want to save yourself from the clutches of these visions and spectres, believe me, believe what I say and do as I command.

GUIMARD: You don't need to ask that of me, I find everything *is* as you say!

BISKRA: Now you see, idolater!

GUIMARD: Idolater?

BISKRA: Yes! Show me the idol you're wearing around your neck!

GUIMARD *(takes out a medallion.)*

BISKRA: Crush it under your feet, and call upon the name of God, the Most Compassionate, the Most Merciful.

GUIMARD *(hesitantly)*: My patron saint Edward, King and martyr.

BISKRA: Can he protect you? Can he?

GUIMARD: No, he can't! – *(Wakes up.)* Yes, he can!

BISKRA: Let's see then! *(Opens the door, the fabric flaps and the grass scatters.)*

GUIMARD *(covers his mouth)*: Close the door!

BISKRA: Cast off your false idol!

GUIMARD: No, I can't!

BISKRA: Look! The Simoom won't touch a hair on my head, but you, infidel, he will kill! Cast off your false idol!

GUIMARD *(casts the medallion on the floor)*: Water! I'm dying!

BISKRA: Pray to God, the One God, the Most Compassionate, the Most Merciful.

GUIMARD: What shall I pray?

BISKRA: Repeat after me!

GUIMARD: Speak!

BISKRA: There is no god but the one God. In the name of God, the Most Compassionate, the Most Merciful!

GUIMARD: "There is no god but the one God. In the name of God, the Most Compassionate, the Most Merciful!"

BISKRA: Lie down on the ground!

GUIMARD *(lies down reluctantly.)*

BISKRA: What can you hear?

GUIMARD: I hear a spring murmur!

BISKRA: You see! God is One and there is no other. He, the Most Compassionate, the Most Merciful! What do you see?

GUIMARD: I see a spring murmur – I hear a lamp shine – in a

window with green shutters – by a white street –

BISKRA: Who sits by the window?

GUIMARD: My wife – Elise!

BISKRA: Who's standing behind the curtain, placing his hand upon her neck? –

GUIMARD: It's my son – Georges!

BISKRA: How old is your son?

GUIMARD: Four years at St Nicolas-tide!

BISKRA: And can he already stand behind the curtain with his hand upon the neck of another man's wife?

GUIMARD: No he can't – but it *is* him!

BISKRA: Four years old with a blond moustache!

GUIMARD: A blond moustache, you say! – Ah, that's – Jules, my friend!

BISKRA: Standing behind the curtain with his hand around your wife's neck!

GUIMARD: The devil!

BISKRA: Do you see your son?

GUIMARD: No, not anymore!

BISKRA *(imitates the sound of bells ringing on her guitar):* What do you see now?

GUIMARD: I see bells ringing – and my mouth tastes of rotting corpses – it reeks like rancid butter – Urgh! –

BISKRA: Can't you hear the priest lamenting the death of a child?

GUIMARD: Wait a moment! – I can't hear it – *(with sadness)* but is that what you wish? – well – now I hear it!

BISKRA: Do you see the wreath on the coffin they carry between them?

GUIMARD: Yes –

BISKRA: See the violet ribbons – printed with silver letters – "Farewell, my beloved Georges – Your Father".

GUIMARD: Yes, that's what it says! – *(Weeps.)* My Georges! Georges! My beloved child! – Elise, my wife, comfort me! – Help me! *(Gropes around.)* Where are you? Elise! Have you left me? Answer! Call your beloved's name!

A VOICE *(from the roof)*: Jules! Jules!

GUIMARD: Jules!? But my name is – What is my name? Charles is my name! – And she called Jules! Elise – beloved wife – answer me! Your spirit is here, I feel it – and you promised never to love another!

(The voice laughs.)

GUIMARD: Who's laughing?

BISKRA: Elise! Your wife!

GUIMARD: Kill me! – I don't want to live any longer! Life disgusts me like sauerkraut in Saint-Doux – You don't know what Saint-Doux is, do you? It's pork-lard! *(Spits.)* I have no saliva left – water! Water! Or I'll bite you!

(A full storm rages outside.)

BISKRA *(covers her mouth and coughs)*: Now you die, Frenchman! Write your last will while there is still time! – Where is your journal?

GUIMARD *(takes out his journal and a pen)*: What shall I write?!

BISKRA: A husband thinks of his wife when he is about to die – and of his children!

GUIMARD *(writes)*: "Elise – I curse you! Simoom – I'm dying – "

BISKRA: Sign it or your testament is not valid!

GUIMARD: How shall I sign?

BISKRA: Write "La ilaha illa Allah"!

GUIMARD *(writes)*: It is written! May I die now?

BISKRA: Now you may die, like a cowardly soldier who has deserted his people! And you'll have a terrific funeral with the jackals to lament your death! *(Drums an attack on the guitar.)* Can you hear the drum rolls? Attack! – The infidels, with the sun and Simoom on their side – advance – from the hide-outs! *(Strums the guitar.)* The shots are fired all along the front – the French can't reload – the Arab ranks strike – the French flee! –

GUIMARD *(gets up)*: The French never flee!

BISKRA *(sounds the retreat on a flute she has taken from her cloak)*: The French flee, when retreat is sounded!

GUIMARD: They are retreating – it's the retreat – and I'm here – *(He tears off his epaulettes.)* I'm dead! *(Collapses on the ground.)*

BISKRA: Yes you are dead! – You don't know it, but you've been dead for a long time! – *(Goes to the charnel house, picks up a skull.)*

GUIMARD: Have I been dead? *(Touches his face.)*

BISKRA: For a long, long time! – Look in the mirror! *(She shows him the skull.)*

GUIMARD: Ah! That's me!

BISKRA: Don't you see how your cheeks are hollowed? Or how the vultures have gorged on your eyes? Don't you recognise the hole left behind by the wisdom tooth you had pulled out? Or the cleft in your chin where that pretty little beard grew, the one your Elise liked to stroke? Don't you see where the ear was, the one your Georges used to kiss in the morning at the breakfast table? Don't you see where the axe severed your neck – when the executioner put the deserter to death?! –

GUIMARD *(who has taken it all in, in horror, falls down dead.)*

BISKRA *(who has been kneeling, rises whilst checking his pulse. she sings)*: Simoom! Simoom! *(Opens the door, the fabric flaps, she covers her mouth and collapses.)* Youssef!

Scene three

AS BEFORE. YOUSSEF *(coming up from the basement.)*

YOUSSEF *(examines Guimard, looks for Biskra)*: Biskra! *(Catches sight of Biskra, lifts her up into his arms.)* Are you alive?

BISKRA: Is the Frenchman dead?

YOUSSEF: If he's not, he soon will be! Simoom! Simoom!

BISKRA: Then I'm alive! But give me water!

YOUSSEF *(carries her towards the trap-door)*: Here! – Now Youssef is yours!

BISKRA: And Biskra will be the mother of your son! Youssef, great Youssef!

YOUSSEF: Biskra the Strong! Stronger than Simoom!

Curtain

Translators' Note

For such a short play, Simoom is remarkably multi-layered. It is ripe for a post-modern interpretation and its central conflict could easily be transposed to a contemporary setting. Strindberg set the play in Algeria, during a period in which relations between native Algerians and French settlers were tense. He states that the play is set 'in our time'. For the modern reader, this 'in our time', provides an ambiguity that allows for resonances with other, later conflicts. For the modern reader, or indeed, the translator, parallels might be drawn with later conflicts – not only between France and Algeria, but also in other North African countries, or even the fraught relationships between 'Allied Forces' in Iraq and Afghanistan and the militias or civilians in those countries.

We did consider setting our translation of the play within this modern political discourse, but decided that such a leap, while interesting, would be too loaded – we didn't want to overly impose our interpretation of what Strindberg was trying to do with his play. It is not clear how important the political aspect was for Strindberg. Perhaps the purpose of the conflict was rather to heighten the psychological power – foregrounding the female lead Biskra's hatred and the mystical, other-worldly atmosphere that creates. In this respect, the play is more a pastiche on the psychological horror and Gothic style of Edgar Allan Poe. It certainly employs an exoticism that to a contemporary Scandinavian audience would have further underlined the magic, mysterious powers this Arabic character possesses.

Another challenge we encountered was the difficulty of understanding how Strindberg related to Islam. It is clear that the contrast between the French soldier Guimard's Catholicism, and Biskra and Youssef's Muslim faith is significant. It heightens the relationship between the imperialist and the oppressed, and adds an additional mystical element to Biskra's powers of suggestion over Guimard (bearing in mind the contemporary audience). It appeared to us that Strindberg consciously used Muslim terminology in the prayers and incantations included in the play. However, it was not clear to what extent these were taken from contemporary translations of Islamic texts, or 'created' from Strindberg's knowledge or perception of Islam.

For this reason, we decided not to try and reproduce the prayers in English as they would be spoken by a Muslim today. Instead we translated them very close to the original, but using certain terms that would render the religious associations of the texts recognisable to an English-speaking audience.

We were intrigued by the gender relations in Simoom and how the play could be read from a gender perspective. Biskra, a young woman, is disguised throughout the play as a young man: Ali, the guide who has recently died at the hands of the French. The disguise is so effective that Guimard really believes, even while he is being driven to his death in the Marabout, that he is there with Ali. It is to a man that he begs for salvation, and it is Biskra, a woman, who deceives him and ultimately ends his life. The strength of this male/female character is interesting to consider in light of Strindberg's fabled misogyny, and the more common characterisation by Strindberg of women as hysterical and untrustworthy. Biskra, as the anti-hero of Simoom, is powerful and cunning in her torture of Guimard, and, through her powers, deserving of her lover Youssef's respect. However, the fact that she needs to dress up as a man to achieve a position of trust with the Frenchman still reflects the ambiguity of Strindberg's opinions of women, and indeed the complex gender roles of the time.

Nichola Smalley and Anna Tebelius

Facing Death

(1892)

Translated from the Swedish
by Nichola Smalley and Anna Tebelius

CAST

MONSIEUR DURAND, guesthouse owner, former civil servant at the State Railways
ADÈLE, his daughter, 27 years of age
ANNETTE, daughter, 24
THÉRÈSE, daughter, 18
ANTONIO, lieutenant with an Italian cavalry regiment

In French Switzerland, during the 1880s.

A dining room with a long table. Through the open door in the wall at the back, visible just above the cypresses in the churchyard, are Lac Leman, with the Savoy Alps and the French spa town, Evian. A door to the kitchen stage left. A door leading to the living quarters stage right.

Scene one

MONSIEUR DURAND. ADÈLE.

MONSIEUR DURAND *(stands with binoculars, surveying the lake.)*
ADÈLE *(enters from the kitchen, wearing an apron and with her sleeves rolled up; she carries a tray with the coffee things.)*: Haven't you fetched the pastries yet, father?

DURAND: No, I sent Pierre today. These last few days my chest has been so bad I can't make it up the steep hill.

ADÈLE: Pierre again! That will cost us three sous! Where d'you suppose we'll find them, when there's been only one guest staying these last two months.

DURAND: That much is true, I really think Annette should be the one fetching the pastries.

ADÈLE: Well that would really destroy this house's reputation, but then that's what you've been doing all along!

DURAND: Not you too, Adèle!

ADÈLE: Yes, I too have wearied. I resisted for as long as I could, longer than anyone else!

DURAND: Yes, you did, and you kept your humanity, when Thérèse and Annette tortured me. Since mother died it's you and I who have kept this house going. Just like Cinderella, you were forced to slave in the kitchen, and I took care of the service, the sweeping, the cleaning, lighting the fires, running errands. If you're tired, how do you think I feel?

ADÈLE: But you're not allowed to be tired, not when you have whittled down the dowry of your three unmarried children!

DURAND *(suddenly hears something)*: Can you hear ringing and drumming down at Cully?! If there's a fire, they will surely perish – the Föhn wind is about to whip up, I can see it on the lake.

ADÈLE: Well, have you paid the fire insurance on our house?

DURAND: Yes, of course I have, or I could never have got the last mortgage.

ADÈLE: How much remains unencumbered?

DURAND: A fifth of the value of the fire insurance. But you know

how the value of my property has fallen since the railway was moved eastwards, away from our front door.
ADÈLE: All the more welcome, then!...
DURAND *(harshly)*: Adèle! *(Pause.)* Will you put out the stove?
ADÈLE: Impossible before the pastries have arrived!
DURAND: Well, here they are now!

Scene two

THE FORMER. PIERRE *(with a basket)*. ADÈLE.

ADÈLE *(inspects the basket)*: No pastries! Just a bill! Two, three!
PIERRE: Yeah, the baker said he ain't gonna give you any more before he's been paid. – Then I passed the butcher and the grocer, who put these bills my way. *(Exits.)*
ADÈLE: Oh dear God, that's the end of us – but what's this? *(Opens a package.)*
DURAND: Candles I purchased for the mass in honour of my beloved René. It happens to be the anniversary of his death today.
ADÈLE: So you can afford things like that, can you?!
DURAND: Yes, paid for with tips I earned. Don't you think it's humiliating enough for me, to have to hold out my hand when a guest leaves... Why can't you grant me the one satisfaction I still possess, to just once a year indulge my own sorrow! To relive the memory of the most precious thing life gave me.
ADÈLE: If only he were alive now, then you'd see how precious he was!
DURAND: It's very possible there's a grain of truth in your irony... the way I remember him, however, he wasn't as you are now!
ADÈLE: Kindly receive Monsieur Antonio yourself, then, when he comes down for his coffee without pastries! – Oh! If only mother had been alive; she always knew what to do when you were at a loss!
DURAND: Your mother had her talents!

ADÈLE: Even though you only saw faults!
DURAND: Monsieur Antonio is arriving! – Run along now, and I'll speak with him!
ADÈLE: It would be better if you went out to borrow money so we could be spared the scandal!
DURAND: I can't borrow a sous! After ten years of borrowing! Let everything crash at once, everything, at least that would be the end of it!
ADÈLE: The end for you, yes! But you never think of us!
DURAND: No, I've never thought of you! Never!
ADÈLE: Are you asking me to be grateful for our upbringing again?
DURAND: Merely responding to an unjust accusation! Leave now, I'll face the storm, as per usual.
ADÈLE: As per usual! Hm! *(Exits.)*

Scene three

MONSIEUR DURAND. ANTONIO.

ANTONIO *(from the back of the stage)*: Good morning, Monsieur Durand.
DURAND: Has Monsieur Lieutenant already been out for a walk?
ANTONIO: Yes, I was down near Cully, watching a chimney fire being put out! – And now I'm really looking forward to my coffee and pastry!
DURAND: I need not tell you how embarrassing this is for me, but I must advise you that due to lack of funds, this house can no longer remain in business.
ANTONIO: How so?
DURAND: To be quite frank, we are bankrupt!
ANTONIO: But my dear Monsieur Durand, is there no chance I could assist you in this, I hope, temporary inconvenience?
DURAND: No, there's no chance, and the position of the house has been so fundamentally undermined during the last few years, that I'd rather see it all collapse now, than be

suspended indefinitely in a state of anxiety over what must come!

ANTONIO: I still believe you're being too gloomy.

DURAND: I don't know on what basis you dare to doubt my statements!

ANTONIO: Because I want to help you.

DURAND: I don't want any help! Hard times will teach my children, once and for all, to lead a different life than this life of frivolity. Apart from Adèle, who really takes care of the kitchen, what do the others do? Play and sing, stroll about and flirt; and as long as there's a crust in the house, I doubt they'll ever do anything useful!

ANTONIO: That may be, but while the state of your affairs is being investigated, we must have food in this house! Allow me to stay another month, and I'll give you my rent in advance.

DURAND: I thank you, but no, we must ride this train to the end of the line, even if it derails us. And I have no wish to continue a business which bears no fruit, only humiliation. Imagine, last spring, the house had been empty for three months. Finally, an American family arrived and saved us. The morning after their arrival, what should I see on the stairwell, but the son clutching my daughter – it was Thérèse – about to kiss her! What would you have done in my place?

ANTONIO *(embarrassed)*: I don't know...

DURAND: I know what I, as a father, should have done – but, as a father I didn't do it! Next time, I know what I'll do!

ANTONIO: It seems to me, for that reason in particular, that you should pay attention to what you're doing, and not leave your daughters to their fates...

DURAND: Monsieur Antonio... You're a young man, for whom I have, for some inexplicable reason, developed an affinity. Whether you value that or not, I beg of you one thing: do not offer any opinions about my person or my actions.

ANTONIO: Monsieur Durand, that I can promise, if you'd only answer one question: are you Swiss-born, or not?

DURAND: I am a citizen of Switzerland.

ANTONIO: That much I know, but I'm asking if you were born in Switzerland.

DURAND *(uncertain)*: Yes!

ANTONIO: I only ask out of interest. In any case, since I'm forced to believe you when you say that the guest house is closing, I want to repay my debt. It's only ten francs, but I can hardly leave with unfinished business.

DURAND: I'm not sure whether this is a real debt, as I'm not responsible for the accounts, but if you've deceived me, you'll answer for it. Now I'll go and buy pastries. Then we'll see. *(Exits.)*

Scene four

ANTONIO. *Presently* THÉRÈSE *(with a mouse-trap in her hand, in her dressing gown with her hair loose). Later* ADÈLE.

THÉRÈSE: Look, there's Antonio! I thought I heard the old man!

ANTONIO: Yes, he said he'd fetch the pastries, didn't he!

THÉRÈSE: Hasn't he done it yet? No? I've had enough of him!

ANTONIO: You're so beautiful today, Thérèse, but that mouse-trap does nothing for you.

THÉRÈSE: A fine mouse-trap it is too! I've been baiting it for a whole month and not killed a single mouse. Still the bait is gone every morning. – Have you seen Mimmi?

ANTONIO: That damned cat! It always seems to be hanging around somewhere! But today I've been blessed by its absence.

THÉRÈSE: You mustn't speak harshly of absent friends. And remember – he who loves me loves my cat. *(Puts the mousetrap on the table and removes an empty saucer from underneath the table.)* Adèle! – Adèle!

ADÈLE *(in the kitchen doorway)*: What does her highness command so loudly?

THÉRÈSE: I command milk for my cat, and a rind of cheese for your mice!

ADÈLE: Go and find it yourself.

THÉRÈSE: Is that a fitting answer for her highness?

ADÈLE: It's as good an answer as you're going to get! And you should be ashamed for showing yourself among strangers with your hair unbrushed!

THÉRÈSE: We're all old friends here, and... Antonio, go and flatter aunty Adèle and you'll get some milk for Mimmi.

ANTONIO *(hesitates.)*

THÉRÈSE: Well, aren't you going to obey?

ANTONIO *(abruptly)*: No!

THÉRÈSE: What kind of talk is that? Do you want a thrashing?

ANTONIO: Be quiet!

THÉRÈSE *(devastated)*: What! What is it?! Are you trying to remind me of my place, my debt and my weakness?

ANTONIO: No, I'm trying to remind you of my place, my debt and my weakness.

ADÈLE *(takes the saucer)*: Dear friends, come on now, stop this banter?! Make amends, and I'll bring you some decent coffee. – *(Exits to the kitchen.)*

THÉRÈSE *(crying to Antonio)*: You've tired of me, Antonio, and you're going to abandon me.

ANTONIO: Don't cry, it makes your eyes so ugly.

THÉRÈSE: Perhaps it will make them as beautiful as Annette's... then...

ANTONIO: Oh, so it's Annette now? Listen here, joking aside, the coffee seems to be taking its time...

THÉRÈSE: A fine husband you'd make, not even able to wait a moment for the coffee to be ready.

ANTONIO: And what a darling wife you'd make, nagging your husband when you've made a fool of yourself.

Scene five

THE FORMER. ANNETTE *(enters, dressed and with her hair up)*.

ANNETTE: I do believe you're bickering before breakfast!
ANTONIO: Look! There's Annette, already dressed!
THÉRÈSE: Yes, Annette's perfect in every way. And she even has

the advantage of being older than me.

ANNETTE: If you don't hold your tongue...

ANTONIO: Now, now... Be kind, Thérèse. – *(He grabs hold of her waist and kisses her.)*

Scene six

THE FORMER. DURAND.

DURAND *(in doorway. Stops, flabbergasted)*: What's this?

THÉRÈSE *(pulls herself free)*: What?

DURAND: Were my eyes deceiving me?

THÉRÈSE: What did you see?

DURAND: I saw you letting this stranger kiss you.

THÉRÈSE: Lies!

DURAND: Is my sight failing me? Or do you dare to lie to my face?

THÉRÈSE: You're a fine one to talk about lying – you lie to us and to the whole world that you're Swiss by birth, although you're a Frenchman.

DURAND: Who told you that?

THÉRÈSE: Mother did!

DURAND *(to Antonio)*: Monsieur Lieutenant, since our business is now concluded, I would ask you to leave this house straight away! Or else...

ANTONIO: Or else?

DURAND: You may choose your weapon!

ANTONIO: I wonder what kind of weapon you would opt for, apart from the escape route!

DURAND: If I didn't prefer the cane, I'd take my rifle from the last war...

THÉRÈSE: A fine war you fought, deserter!

DURAND: Mother must have said that too! I can't fight against the dead, but I can beat the living to death! *(He lifts his cane and moves towards Antonio.)*

THÉRÈSE and ANNETTE *(hurl themselves between the two men.)*

ANNETTE: Think what you're doing.

THÉRÈSE: You'll end up on the scaffold.

ANTONIO *(steps back)*: Farewell, Monsieur Durand! You may keep my disdain and my ten francs!

DURAND *(takes a gold coin from his waistcoat pocket and throws it after Antonio)*: You bastard, here's your gold, damn you!

THÉRÈSE and ANNETTE *(follow Antonio)*: Don't go! Don't go! Father will kill us!

DURAND *(breaks the cane)*: He who can't kill, will die!

ANTONIO: Farewell! Think of me, the last rat to abandon this sinking ship! *(Exits.)*

Scene seven

THE FORMER, without ANTONIO.

THÉRÈSE *(to Durand)*: So that's the way you treat your guests! Is it any wonder this house is crumbling?

DURAND: Yes, that's the way. With that kind of guest! But tell me, Thérèse, my child... *(Takes her head in his hands.)* My beloved child; tell me, did my eyes deceive me a minute ago, or did you lie to me?

THÉRÈSE *(contrary)*: What?

DURAND: You know what I mean! And it's not so much the thing in itself, which could be quite innocent... it's the question of whether I can trust my own senses that concerns me.

THÉRÈSE: Let's talk of something else instead. Tell me what we're going to eat and drink today! – Anyway, it's a lie that he kissed me!

DURAND: It's not a lie! For heaven's sake, I saw it happen, didn't I?!

THÉRÈSE: Prove it!

DURAND: Prove it! With two witnesses or a policeman! *(to Annette)* Annette my child, will you tell me the truth?

ANNETTE: I saw nothing!

DURAND: That's the correct answer, one should never inform on one's sisters. – You look just like your mother today, Annette!

ANNETTE: Don't say anything bad about mother. Oh, if she had lived to see a day like this!

Scene eight

THE FORMER. ADÈLE.

ADÈLE *(enters with a glass of milk, which she places on the table. Addresses Durand)*: Here's your milk! How did it go with the pastries?

DURAND: The pastries came to nothing, my children, but everything shall be as it used to be.

THÉRÈSE *(snatches the glass from her father)*: You're not to have anything, throwing money away and letting your children starve.

ADÈLE: Has the old wretch been throwing money away? They should have put him in the madhouse when mother said he was ripe for it! Look! Here's another bill that's just come in through the back door!

DURAND *(looks at the bill with a start; then fills a glass of water and downs it in one; takes a seat, and lights a pipe.)*

ANNETTE: And yet he can afford to smoke tobacco?

DURAND *(tired and resigned)*: Dear children, this tobacco has cost no more than the water, it was given to me as a gift months ago! Don't excite yourselves for no reason.

THÉRÈSE *(takes the matches)*: Well, you're not to waste the matches, in any case...

DURAND: If only you knew, Thérèse, how many matches I've wasted on you, rising in the dead of night to make sure you hadn't thrown off your blankets; if only you knew, Annette, how many times I secretly gave you water, when you were crying of thirst, because your mother had some notion that drinking was bad for children.

THÉRÈSE: That was so long ago, I don't care about it. Anyway, it was only your duty, you said so yourself.

DURAND: Yes, that's true, but I did fulfill my duty. And a bit more too!

ADÈLE: Why stop now! Otherwise, who knows what will become

of us! Three young girls, left to fend for ourselves, without a penny to get by on. You do know what desperation can drive one to?

DURAND: I said that ten years ago, but no one would listen; and twenty years ago, I predicted that this moment would come, but I've not been able to stop it coming. I've sat like a lone brakesman on a speeding train, getting closer and closer to the abyss, not able to reach the engine levers to make it stop.

THÉRÈSE: And now you expect thanks for derailing us!

DURAND: No, my child, I'm only asking you to be a little less vicious towards me. You have cream for the cat, but you won't spare a drop of milk for your old man, who has not eaten in... so long.

THÉRÈSE: So it was you who denied the cat her milk!

DURAND: Yes, it was me!

ANNETTE: And perhaps he was the one who ate the morsels we left for the mice!

DURAND: Yes, it was him!

ADÈLE: What a swine! –

THÉRÈSE *(laughs):* Imagine if there'd been poison on it!

DURAND: You mean, if only there had been!

THÉRÈSE: Well, you wouldn't have minded, you who babble on about wanting to shoot yourself, but never do!

DURAND: 'Why haven't you shot yourself?' That's quite a reproach! Well, I'll tell you why I've not done it! Because, my beloved children, I didn't want you to fall on hard times!... Say something nasty to me now! It's like music to my ears, familiar notes... from the good old days...

ADÈLE: Stop that talk, there's no point. Do something! Do something!

THÉRÈSE: Do you know what the consequences would be, if you left us like this?

DURAND: That you'd prostitute yourselves, I imagine. That's what your mother always said, when she'd spent the household money on the lottery.

ADÈLE: Quiet! Not another word about our dear, beloved mother!

DURAND *(singsong, to himself)*: In this house I light, a candle so bright, and when it's aflame, achieved is my aim! And then comes the Föhn with a mighty möhn! Oh I mean moan! Yes! – No! –

(The wind has risen outside and clouds cover the sky.)

DURAND *(springs up; addresses Adèle)*: Put out the stove! The Föhn is coming!

ADÈLE *(looks Durand in the eye)*: There's no Föhn!

DURAND: Put out the stove! If the fire starts there, we'll get nothing on the insurance. Put the stove out, I say! Put it out!

ADÈLE: I don't understand.

DURAND *(looks her in the eyes and takes her hands)*: Just obey me! Do as I say!

ADÈLE *(goes out into the kitchen; leaving the door open.)*

DURAND *(to Thérèse and Annette)*: Go upstairs and shut your windows children, and close the chimney flues! But come over here and kiss me first, for I'm going away – – to get you money!

THÉRÈSE: Can you get money?

DURAND: I have a life insurance that I intend to cash in.

THÉRÈSE: How much will you get for it?

DURAND: Six hundred francs if I sell it and five thousand if I die.

THÉRÈSE *(looks anxious.)*

DURAND: Speak your mind, my child! – No, we mustn't be unnecessarily cruel. – Tell me Thérèse, are you so fond of Antonio that you'd be quite unhappy if you didn't get him?

THÉRÈSE: Oh yes!

DURAND: Then you should marry him, if he feels the same about you! But you mustn't be cruel to him, it will only make you unhappy! – Farewell, my dear, dear child! *(Embraces her and kisses her cheeks.)*

THÉRÈSE: You can't die father! You just can't!

DURAND: Will you not grant me peace?

THÉRÈSE: Yes, if that's what you wish! ... Father, forgive me for all the times I've been mean to you.

DURAND: It was nothing, child!

THÉRÈSE: But no one was as mean to you as I!

DURAND: I noticed it less, because I loved you more, although I don't know why. There there, go and shut your windows.
THÉRÈSE: Here are your matches papa! – – And – your milk!
DURAND *(smiles)*: Oh, my child!
THÉRÈSE: Yes, what am I to do! I have nothing else to give you.
DURAND: You gave me so much joy as a child that you owe me nothing. Go now! Just give me a smile like you used to!
THÉRÈSE *(As she goes she turns and throws herself into his arms.)*
DURAND: There, there, my child, that's enough!
(Thérèse runs out.)

Scene nine

MONSIEUR DURAND. ANNETTE. Later ADÈLE.

DURAND: Farewell, Annette!
ANNETTE: Are you going away? I don't understand all this.
DURAND: Yes I'm going away.
ANNETTE: But you will come back, Papa?
DURAND: No one can say whether they will live to see another day, and anyway, there's no harm in saying goodbye.
ANNETTE: Farewell to you then, father! And good luck on your travels! You won't forget to buy us something, like you used to? *(Exits.)*
DURAND: Ah, you remember, even though it's such a long time since I've bought something for you children! Farewell, dear Annette! *(Singsong, to himself.)* For good and ill, do what you will, and where you've sown, shall others reap.
ADÈLE *(enters.)*
DURAND: Adèle! Now listen to me and take note! – If I don't speak plainly, it's only because I want to spare your conscience from knowing too much. – Don't worry, I've sent the children up to their rooms. To begin with, I want you to ask me "Have you any life insurance?" Well!
ADÈLE *(curious, doubtful)*: "Have you any life insurance?"
DURAND: No, I did have, but it was sold long ago, as it seemed to me, that someone was becoming a little too impatient to

benefit from it. – On the other hand, we're insured against fire! Look, here are the documents; hide them well! Now I'll ask you: Do you know how many mass candles you can get for 75 centimes?

ADÈLE: Six.

DURAND *(gestures towards the package of candles)*: How many candles can you see there?

ADÈLE: Only five!

DURAND: That's because the sixth is hidden somewhere out of reach, but just close enough! –

ADÈLE: Christ!

DURAND *(takes out his watch)*: In about five minutes everything will be reduced to ashes!

ADÈLE: No!

DURAND: Yes! Can you see any other light in all this darkness? No! – So! – That's the business taken care of. Now to something else! If Mr. Durand leaves this life as an *(whispers)* arsonist, it's all the same, but that he lived his life up until that point as an honourable man, that's something his children should know. – Well, perhaps I was born in France – There was no need to tell that bastard! – Just before I was old enough to be enlisted, I fell in love with the woman who was to become my wife. In order to marry, we travelled here and were naturalised! – When the last war broke out and it seemed as though I would have to take up arms against my own country, I came out as an irregular against the Germans! – As you can hear, I've never deserted: the story was a fabrication of your mother's!

ADÈLE: My mother never lied!

DURAND: There! Now the corpse has risen and stands between us again! I can't argue with the dead, but I swear I'm telling the truth. Take note! And as regards your dowry, and indeed your inheritance from your mother, the connection is as follows: to begin with, she so comprehensively wasted my inheritance through greed and unwise speculation, that I was forced to resign from my vocation and set up this guest house. Furthermore, some of her inheritance went towards your upbringing and that can hardly be said to be wasted. – So that was also untrue...

ADÈLE: No, that's not what mother said on her deathbed...

DURAND: Then your mother lied, even on her deathbed, as she had done throughout her life... And that's the curse that has followed me like a phantom! Think how much you have made me suffer through the years with these two lies! I had no wish to trouble your young minds and make you doubt your mother's integrity, so I held my tongue. I have borne her cross throughout our married life; I bore the weight of all her failings, bore the brunt of her mistakes, until finally even I believed I was the guilty one. And she wasn't slow to believe herself guiltless, at first, and then, the victim! "Blame it on me" was what I always said when she found herself in a tight spot. And she did! And I bore it! But the more she became indebted to me, the more she hated me with the full force of that boundless hate borne of obligation, and finally she despised me, in order to reinforce the illusion that she had fooled me! In the end, she taught you to despise me, because she needed an ally in her weakness! I believed and hoped that this cruel but weak soul would die when she died; but cruelty lives and grows like a cancer – first the healthy parts are stunted and then they wither. And when I tried to change all that was wrong in the ways of this house, I was met with: "mother" – "that's what mother said" and therefore it is so; "that's how mother would do it" and therefore it's right! And to you, I became someone worthy of pity when I was kind, worthy of contempt when I was discreet, worthy of disgust when you got your way and ruined this house!

ADÈLE: How honorable of you to accuse the dead who aren't here to defend themselves!

DURAND *(speaks very quickly and with exaltation):* I'm not dead yet, but I soon will be! Will you defend me then? – No you don't need to! But defend your sisters. Think only of my children, Adèle. Care for Thérèse as a mother would. She's the youngest and the liveliest, quick to cruelty and to kindness, impulsive but weak! Make sure she marries soon, if you can arrange it! – Now you can smell the hay burning!

ADÈLE: Good Lord, save us!

DURAND *(takes a drink from the glass of water):* He will! – And for Annette you should find a teaching position! That way she'll get out into the world and into good company. – When you receive the money, I want you to take care of it. Don't be mean, provide for your sisters, so they are presentable in society! – Save nothing but the family papers, which are in my bureau, in the middle drawer. Here's the key. – You have the fire insurance. - - - *(Smoke can be seen coming in through the ceiling.)* Now it's almost done! In a moment the bells of St. François will ring! – Promise me one thing. – Never a word of this to your sisters! It would only disturb their peaceful lives. *(He takes a seat at the table.)* And one more thing: never a harsh word about their mother! You'll find her portrait in the bureau as well – I never told you, as I thought it enough that she was constantly here in spirit! – Give my love to Thérèse and tell her to forgive me! Don't forget that she's to have the very best when you buy clothes, you know how she is with such things, and you know where her weakness might lead her!... Tell Annette...

(A muted sound of bells from without. The smoke thickens. Monsieur Durand drops his head onto his hands on the table.)

ADÈLE: Fire! – Fire! – Father! – What's wrong with you? You'll burn! –

DURAND *(lifts his head and pushes away the glass with a meaningful gesture.)*

ADÈLE: You've... taken... poison!

DURAND *(nods in confirmation)*: You have the insurance documents? – Tell Thérèse... and Annette...

(His head falls forwards again. Another ringing of bells; noise and commotion off-stage.)

Curtain

Translators' Note

It is interesting to note how Strindberg's writing remains up-to-date. Like Simoom, Facing Death has several contemporary parallels. The economic difficulties faced by the family and the desperation it leads to for the main male character, M. Durand, could easily be compared to our 21st Century recession and the economic hardship many families are struggling with throughout Europe and around the world. The relationships between M. Durand, his daughters and with his deceased wife and their mother are also interesting to note for their potential crossover into an analysis based on contemporary gender discourse and in relation to Strindberg's own views on women. Once again, we considered re-locating the play to a more contemporary setting in order to explore the ramifications of this in a modern context, but couldn't see how to do this without making it overly literal.

Suicide is a dominant theme in *Facing Death* (and in Simoom, but there it is framed differently). We detected echoes of Shakespeare's King Lear in the suicide of M. Durand, and in his tragic relationship with his three daughters. Attempting to translate this into the text was challenging, however, and we made the decision to leave it up to interpretation. This reference does indicate Strindberg's indebtedness to literary history, so we thought it was interesting to draw attention it to here.

There is also a second, more subtle, textual reference to Shakespeare in the opening scene, during an argument between M. Durand and his daughter Adele. The Swedish "Även du, Adèle!", which we translated with "Not you too, Adele!", is a reference to Caesar's last word to his betrayer Brutus, most famously used by Shakespeare (although it is said to pre-date him). We chose our translation over more semantically literal phrases such as 'You too, Adele?', as we found, when reading it aloud, that the meaning was too easily lost in the more literal translation. Given that this is a text written to be performed, it seemed important to avoid creating a text that could confuse an audience!

M. Durand's descent into madness did provide a few stumbling blocks for our translation as we worked on it. Durand's voice as he babbles to himself in rhyme proved particularly challenging, as we had to find a suitable rhyming couplet to replace it, without losing the mistake made by Durand which so bizarrely signals his delirium. It was also a challenge to find the correct balance of formality/informality between the characters. There is a tendency, when translating texts written in the past, to over-formalise the speech. In a drama translation especially, this can make the dialogue seem stiff and unidiomatic. However, making the dialogue overly informal would mean that some of the tension in the dialogues might be lost. Additionally, it was important to distinguish between the different interlocutors – Durand's inane babbling, Thérèse's childish spitefulness and Antonio's charming recriminations. We tried to do this through our choice of words, creating a distinctive voice for each character, and we hope you can detect the characters' personalities in their voices.

Nichola Smalley and Anna Tebelius

The Bond

(1892)

Translated from the Swedish
by Agnes Broomé and Mathelinda Nabugodi

CAST

CIRCUIT JUDGE, 27 years of age
PASTOR, 60
BARON, 42
BARONESS, 40
PANEL OF TWELVE LAY MAGISTRATES
CLERK OF THE COURT
SHERIFF
CONSTABLE
LAWYER
ALEXANDERSSON, a freeholder
ALMA JONSSON, a house maid
MILKMAID
THRESHER
SPECTATORS

A court room. Door and windows upstage. The cemetery and the church clock tower can be seen through the windows. There is a door stage right. A desk which serves as the Bench stands on a dais stage left. It is decorated with gilded representations of the sword and scales of Justice. On either side of the Bench, chairs and tables have been set out for the Magistrates. There are seats for the public centre stage. The walls are lined with heavy cabinets, on the doors of which hang land taxation notices and official announcements.

The Bond

Scene one

SHERIFF. CONSTABLE.

SHERIFF: Have you ever seen this many people at a summer sessions?

CONSTABLE: No, not in the last fifteen years, not since the notorious Alsjö murders.

SHERIFF: Well, I believe this case may well be as sensational as when that man murdered his parents. It's bad enough that the Baron and Baroness are getting divorced, but when families start wrangling over possessions and land, all hell breaks loose. All that's missing now is that they contest the custody of their only child, then King Solomon himself couldn't pass judgement.

CONSTABLE: Yes, what about that? Some say this and some say that, but surely someone must be to blame?

SHERIFF: Not necessarily: sometimes it's nobody's fault that two people quarrel, and other times it's only one person's fault that both fight. Take my old battleaxe; she stomps about in a fury even when I'm not there, or so I'm told. Besides, this is no quarrel but a fully-fledged criminal case and in most of those, one party is the plaintiff, who has been wronged, and the other the defendant, or the criminal. It's hard to know who the guilty one is in this case since both parties are plaintiffs and both defendants!

CONSTABLE: Indeed! These are strange times; it's as if all women have lost their minds. My old lady gets herself worked up, complaining that if life were fair, I should give birth to children, as if our Lord didn't know what He was doing when He created His people. And I get long rants about her being human too, as if I didn't know that already or ever claimed otherwise; and that she has no desire to be my maid, even though in fact I'm her servant.

SHERIFF: Well now. So that plague has caught on in your house, too. My wife reads a paper that she gets up at the manor, and then she tells me, as if it were quite extraordinary, that some woman has started laying bricks, or that some crone has attacked and battered her sick husband. I don't know what the meaning of it is, but she seems angry with me for being a man!

CONSTABLE: Yes, quite extraordinary. *(Offers snuff.)* Beautiful weather! The rye stands shoulder-high and the risk of frost has passed.

SHERIFF: I've no crops in the ground myself and good years are bad years for me: no repossessions, no auctions. Do you know the new Judge who's presiding today?

CONSTABLE: No, but they say he's young and only just qualified; this is his first time on the Bench…

SHERIFF: And he's supposed to be a bit of a Pietist. Hm.

CONSTABLE: Hm, hm. The court sermon's taking a long time today.

SHERIFF *(places a large Bible on the Clerk's desk and twelve smaller ones for the Magistrates)*: It can't be long now; they've been at it for almost an hour.

CONSTABLE: He's quite a preacher, the Pastor, once he gets going. *(Pause.)* Will the spouses appear in court?

SHERIFF: Yes, both of them, so there's bound to be some commotion… *(The church bells start to ring.)* There, it's finally over! – Tidy the desk a bit, and then I think we can begin.

CONSTABLE: And the inkwells have been filled?

Scene Two

AS BEFORE. BARON. BARONESS.

BARON *(softly to the Baroness)*: So, before we embark on our year of separation, we're fully agreed on all counts. Firstly, no recriminations before the court?

BARONESS: Do you think I want to stand here and expose every intimate detail of our married life to a prying bunch of peasants?

BARON: Good. Further: you'll keep the child during the separation, on the condition that the boy may visit me whenever I please, and that he's raised according to the principles I've drawn up, and which you've approved?

BARONESS: Indeed.

BARON: And I'll provide you and the child with three thousand kronor from the estate revenue during the separation period?

BARONESS: Agreed.

BARON: Then I've nothing more to add, except to bid you farewell! Only you and I know why we're parting and for the sake of our son, no one else needs to know. And for his sake I also implore you: don't start a fight and provoke us into smearing his parents' good names. Even without that, this cruel world will likely make him pay dearly for his parents' divorce.

BARONESS: I won't start a fight as long as I get to keep my child!

BARON: Then let's focus our concern solely on his welfare and forget what has passed between us. And remember this: if we quarrel over the child and contest each other's parental ability, the Judge can rule us both unsuitable and place the boy with Pietists to be raised in hatred and contempt of his parents!

BARONESS: That's impossible!

BARON: No, my friend, such is the law.

BARONESS: It's a stupid law!

BARON: That may be, but it's the law and it applies to you too.

BARONESS: It's unnatural! And I would never submit to it!

BARON: Nor will you have to since we've decided not to accuse each other. We've never agreed on anything before, but on this single issue we do: we'll separate without acrimony! *(to the Sheriff)* May the Baroness wait in that chamber?

SHERIFF: By all means.

(The Baron accompanies the Baroness to the door stage right, after which he exits through the door upstage.)

Scene Three

SHERIFF. CONSTABLE. LAWYER. ALMA JONSSON. MILKMAID. THRESHER.

LAWYER *(to Alma Jonsson)*: My dear: I don't doubt for a second that you stole from your master, but since he has no witnesses to prove it, you're innocent. However, since your master called you a thief in the presence of two witnesses, he's guilty of slander. So now you're the plaintiff and he's the defendant. Remember this rule: a criminal's first duty is to contest everything!

ALMA JONSSON: Yes, but the Judge just said that I'm no criminal, but that my master is.

LAWYER: You're a criminal because you stole, but since you've requested a lawyer, it's my duty to clear you, and to get your master convicted. Therefore, and for the last time: contest everything! *(To the witnesses.)* And witnesses, what testimony should you give? Listen, a good witness sticks to the point. Understand this: the issue is not did Alma steal, it's did Alexandersson call her a thief, because – and note this carefully – Alexandersson doesn't have the right to support his allegation, but we do. The devil alone knows why. But that's none of your concern. So keep your tongues in check and your fingers on the Bible!

MILKMAID: Oh Lord, I'm so afraid; I don't know what to say!

THRESHER: Just say what I say, and you won't be lying.

Scene Four

AS BEFORE. JUDGE. PASTOR.

JUDGE: Thank you for your sermon, Reverend.

PASTOR: The pleasure is mine, your Honour.

JUDGE: So, as you know this is my first session. I've been dreading taking up this profession, which I've been thrown into practically against my will. The laws are so deficient, the legal system so questionable and human nature so riddled with untruth and deceit that I've often wondered how a judge finds the courage to deliver a definitive verdict. And today you've stirred my fears anew!

PASTOR: It's your duty to be conscientious, to be sure, but sentimentality won't do. And given that everything else on this earth is flawed, we should never presume that judges and verdicts can be beyond reproach.

JUDGE: Perhaps, but that doesn't shield me from the boundless responsibility of holding people's destinies in my hands, especially when the words I speak could affect generations. I'm referring specifically to case of the Baron and his wife. I have to ask: you gave the couple their two warnings on behalf of the Parish Council, what's your opinion of their relationship and their relative guilt?

PASTOR: Aha, you want to make me the judge or at least you hope to base your ruling on my testimony. I can only refer you to the minutes of the Parish Council.

JUDGE: Yes, those minutes, I've seen them. But it's precisely what's not in the minutes that I need to find out.

PASTOR: What each spouse has attested privately about the other is confidential. Besides, how am I to know who told the truth and who lied? I can only tell you what I've told them: I don't need to believe one over the other.

JUDGE: But surely you've been able to form an opinion during the hearings, haven't you?

PASTOR: I formed one opinion when I heard one party and a different opinion when I heard the other. In short: I can't make a well-founded assessment of this matter.

JUDGE: But I must give an unequivocal verdict, I who know nothing at all.

PASTOR: Such is the heavy burden of a judge, which I could never bear.

JUDGE: But there must be witnesses? Evidence to be found?

PASTOR: No, the spouses aren't accusing one another publicly. And remember: it only takes two false witnesses to make a case, or one perjurer to break it. Do you think I'd base my verdict on the gossip of kitchen maids, the talk of envious neighbours, or the rancour of vindictive relatives?

JUDGE: Pastor, you're an awful cynic!

PASTOR: That's inevitable, having lived a full sixty years and tended souls for forty. Lying is as ingrained as original sin, and I believe that everybody lies; as children people lie out of fear, when they get older out of self-interest, need, self-preservation. I know those who lie out of pure human kindness. In this case, as far as this couple is concerned, I believe you have your work cut out uncovering who's the more truthful and I just want to warn you not to let yourself be affected by any lurking prejudice. You're newly-wed yourself and therefore under the spell of feminine wiles; for that reason you're naturally inclined to sympathise with an engaging young lady, who's both unhappily married and a mother. On the other hand, you recently became a father, and therefore can't fail to be moved by the father's impending separation from his only child. Beware of pitying either party; pity for one is cruelty toward the other.

JUDGE: But one thing that will lighten my load is that the spouses are agreed in principle.

PASTOR: That's what they all say, but don't rely on it; once they find themselves in front of a judge, it all breaks loose. All that's needed is a little spark and the whole thing is set ablaze! Here come the Magistrates. Goodbye for now. I'll stay, but I'll keep out of sight.

Scene Five

AS BEFORE. THE TWELVE LAY MAGISTRATES. SHERIFF *(rings a bell hanging above the open door upstage. The members of the Court take their seats; spectators fill the room).*

JUDGE: With reference to the provisions of the Code of Judicial Proceedings, Chapter 11, Paragraphs 5, 6 and 8, I hereby declare this Court in session. *(Slowly to the Clerk; then)*: Would

the newly appointed Magistrates please take the oath?
MAGISTRATES *(rise; place their hands on their Bibles and then all speak in unison, except when individual names are spoken)*:
I, Alexander Eklund,
I, Emanuel Wickberg,
I, Karl Johan Sjöberg,
I, Erik Otto Boman,
I, Erenfrid Söderberg,
I, Olof Andersson of Vik,
I, Karl Peter Andersson of Berga,
I, Axel Vallin,
I, Anders Erik Ruth,
I, Sven Oskar Erlin,
I, August Alexander Vass,
I, Ludvig Östman, *(all at once, rhythmically in a low voice)* solemnly promise and swear in the name of God and His Holy Gospel, that I will, to the best of my understanding and in good conscience, do right in every ruling, by the poor man no less than by the rich, and judge in accordance with the law of God and of Sweden, and legal precepts; *(voices growing louder and more assertive)* never to distort the law or promote injustice, for kith or kin, out of envy and spite, or fear, nor for bribes and gifts, nor any other reason, whatever it may be, and not to find him guilty who is guiltless, or guiltless who is guilty. *(Louder.)* Nor will I reveal, to those on trial or others, the deliberations conducted behind closed doors, before a verdict is reached or after. All this I will and shall uphold, as an honest and sincere Magistrate, without malice… *(Pause.)* So help me God! *(The Magistrates take their seats.)*

JUDGE *(to the Sheriff)*: The Court is ready to hear the first case.

August Strindberg

Scene Six

AS BEFORE. LAWYER. ALEXANDERSSON. ALMA JONSSON. MILKMAID. THRESHER.

SHERIFF *(calls)*: Miss Jonsson versus Mr Alexandersson.
LAWYER: I represent the plaintiff, Alma Jonsson.
JUDGE: The housemaid Alma Jonsson has in her suit against her former master Alexandersson sought a conviction according to Chapter 16, Paragraph 8 of the Penal Code, of six months incarceration or a fine, because Alexandersson called her a thief without proving his accusation or instigating legal proceedings against her. What does the defendant have to say?
ALEXANDERSSON: I called her a thief because I saw her steal.
JUDGE: Do you have any witnesses to the theft?
ALEXANDERSSON: No, as it happens I haven't. I mostly keep to myself.
JUDGE: Why didn't you press charges against the girl?
ALEXANDERSSON: Because I don't sue people! And besides we employers don't make a fuss about petty theft, partly because it's so common, partly because we don't want to ruin our servants' future.
JUDGE: What does Alma Jonsson have to say to this?
ALMA JONSSON: Well…
LAWYER: Be quiet! Alma Jonsson, who in this case isn't the defendant but the plaintiff, would like to have her witnesses heard, in order to prove that Alexandersson slandered her.
JUDGE: Since Alexandersson has already confessed to the slander, no witnesses are necessary. However, the Court needs to establish whether Alma Jonsson is guilty of the accusation, because if Alexandersson had just cause for his statement, it would constitute a mitigating factor in the sentencing.
LAWYER: I wish to contest that last statement with reference to the Penal Code, Chapter 16, Paragraph 13, which states

that a person accused of slander is not allowed to submit evidence in support of his allegation.

JUDGE: Claimants, witnesses and members of the public are dismissed so that the Court may deliberate.

(All exit, except the members of the Court.)

Scene Seven

THE COURT.

JUDGE: Is Alexandersson a trustworthy and reliable man?
CLERK: He is.
JUDGE: Is Alma Jonsson known to be an honest maid?
ERIK OTTO BOMAN: She was dismissed for petty theft from my house last year.
JUDGE: And even so I'll have to fine Alexandersson. There's no avoiding it. What are his circumstances?
LUDVIG ÖSTMAN: He's behind on his taxes and his crops failed last year; a fine will break him.
JUDGE: And yet I can find no reason to adjourn the case since the circumstances are clear and Alexandersson isn't allowed to submit evidence. Does anyone object or have anything to add?
ALEXANDER EKLUND: I'd only like to indulge in a general observation: a case like this, where the party who's not only innocent, but injured, is punished and the thief has her so-called honour restored, may easily cause people to become less charitable towards their neighbours and lawsuits may become more common as a result.
JUDGE: That may well be, but such general observations do not belong in the court records, and a verdict must be reached. I'm asking the Panel only whether Alexandersson is guilty according to the Penal Code, Chapter 16, Paragraph 13?
MAGISTRATES: Yes!
JUDGE *(to the Sheriff)*: Call in the parties and witnesses.

August Strindberg

Scene Eight

ALL *(enter.)*

JUDGE: In the case of Miss Jonsson versus Mr Alexandersson, the Court sentences Mr Alexandersson to pay a fine of one hundred kronor for slander.

ALEXANDERSSON: But I caught her stealing! – This is how forbearance is repaid!

LAWYER *(to Alma Jonsson)*: You see; as long as you contest, anything goes! Alexandersson was a fool and didn't contest. If I had been his lawyer, and he had contested the plaintiff's case, then I would soon have challenged your witnesses, and you'd be in the dock! – Let's step outside and settle our business. *(Exits with Alma Jonsson and the witnesses.)*

ALEXANDERSSON *(to the Sheriff)*: And now I suppose I'm to write a reference for Alma, and attest that she's been a good and honest servant.

SHERIFF: That's not my concern.

ALEXANDERSSON *(to the Constable)*: And because of this I'll lose my house and land! So this is how justice is done: the thief gets the honour and the victim the whip! Damn it! – Come by for a drink later, Öman.

CONSTABLE: I'll come by later, but stop shouting.

ALEXANDERSSON: I'm damn well going to shout, even if it cost me three months in jail!

CONSTABLE: Just don't shout. Don't shout.

Scene Nine

AS BEFORE. Then BARON and BARONESS.

JUDGE *(to the Sheriff)*: Call the divorce case between Baron Sprengel and his wife Hélène, born Malmberg.

SHERIFF: The divorce case between Baron Sprengel and his wife Hélène, born Malmberg!

The Bond

BARON and BARONESS *(enter.)*

JUDGE: In the case brought against his wife, Baron Sprengel has declared that he no longer wishes to continue the marriage and requests, since the intervention of the Parish Council has proven fruitless, to be ordered to complete a year's separation of bed and residence. Does the Baroness have any objections?

BARONESS: I don't object to the divorce, provided that I get to keep my child. That's my condition.

JUDGE: The law doesn't recognise any conditions in this case, and the Court will decide in the matter of the child.

BARONESS: That's extraordinary!

JUDGE: And for that reason it's important that the Court learns who provoked the disagreement that caused the divorce. According to the minutes of the Parish Council submitted to the Court it seems that the wife has admitted that she has at times had a combative and difficult temper, while the husband has not taken any guilt upon himself. The Baroness thus seems to have confessed to…

BARONESS: That's a lie!

JUDGE: I find it difficult to believe that the Parish Council's minutes, witnessed by the Pastor and eight other trustworthy men, would be inaccurate.

BARONESS: It's falsely written!

JUDGE: Such outbursts before the Court will not go unpunished.

BARON: I would like it recorded that I've voluntarily ceded the child to the Baroness on certain conditions.

JUDGE: And I repeat once more what I just said: the Court, not the parties, decides the outcome. So: the Baroness denies being the cause of the disagreement?

BARONESS: Yes, I do! And it's not one person's fault that two quarrel!

JUDGE: This isn't a quarrel, but a criminal case, and besides, the Baroness does seem to display a quarrelsome temper and a reckless manner.

BARONESS: Then you don't know my husband.

JUDGE: Please explain yourself; I can't base a verdict on

insinuations.

BARON: In that case I ask for the case to be dismissed, so that I may seek a divorce through other channels.

JUDGE: The case is already in progress and must be heard. – The Baroness has just alleged that the husband is the cause of the divorce. Can this be proven?

BARONESS: Yes, it can!

JUDGE: Then please do so, but consider that this entails annulling the Baron's rights as a father and his right to the estate.

BARONESS: Those he has forfeited many times over, not least when he denied me sleep and nourishment.

BARON: At this point I'm obliged to make it clear that I never denied the Baroness sleep. I merely asked her to not sleep until noon because it left the household neglected and the child without supervision. With regards to food, I've always let the mistress of the house decide and I've only discouraged a couple of extravagant parties, as the mismanaged household wouldn't allow such expenditure.

BARONESS: And he's left me lying ill without calling a doctor.

BARON: The Baroness was in the habit of falling ill whenever she didn't get her way, but this type of illness soon passed. I once called out a specialist from town and he explained to me that it was all affectation, so the next time the Baroness fell ill, simply because her new wall mirror didn't match her aspirations, I chose not to summon the doctor.

JUDGE: Incidents of this nature can't be taken into account in the sentencing of such a serious case. There must be more profound reasons for seeking a divorce.

BARONESS: Surely the Court would consider it grounds for divorce that a father won't allow a mother to raise her child?

BARON: Firstly, the Baroness has let a maid care for the child and whenever the Baroness herself assisted with the care, it always went wrong. Secondly, she sought to raise the boy a woman, not a man; she made him walk around in girl's skirts until he was four years old; even today at the age of eight he has long hair like a girl, he's forced to sew and crochet, and plays with dolls, all of which I consider to be detrimental to the child's normal development into a man. At the same time she would amuse herself by dressing the servants' daughters like boys, cutting their hair short and putting them to work at chores that boys normally do. In short: I took charge of the upbringing of my son once I noticed these deranged symptoms, the consequences of which have been seen to lead to crimes against nature, not to mention Chapter 18 of the Penal Code.

JUDGE: And yet you wish to leave the child in his mother's care?

BARON: Yes, because I've never entertained the cruel notion of separating mother and child, and because the mother promised to change. In any case, my consent was given on the condition that the issue of custody would never go before the Court. But since we're now throwing accusations at each other, I've changed my mind, especially now that I'm the defendant and no longer the plaintiff.

BARONESS: This is how that man keeps his promises.

BARON: My promises, like those of others, have always been conditional, and as long as the conditions have been met, I've kept my promises.

BARONESS: And he promised me personal freedom within the marriage…

BARON: Naturally on the understanding that the laws of decency weren't broken, but when all boundaries were overstepped and freedom had come to conceal license, I considered my promise circumvented.

BARONESS: And he tormented me with the most unreasonable jealousy, which in itself is enough to make married life unbearable. He was even jealous of the doctor, how ridiculous.

BARON: This jealousy consisted of my advice against employing a notorious and indiscreet masseur to handle a condition normally treated by a woman, unless the Baroness is referring to when I threw that inspector out for smoking in my drawing room and offering the Baroness cigars.

BARONESS: Since we've stumbled into shamelessness,

the whole truth might as well come out: the Baron has committed adultery. Is that enough to make him unfit to raise my child?

JUDGE: Can you prove this, Baroness Sprengel?

BARONESS: Yes, I can – here, I have letters!

JUDGE *(accepts the letters)*: How long ago was this?

BARONESS: A year ago.

JUDGE: The time for filing a suit has lapsed, but the incident itself weighs heavily against the Baron and may lose him the right to his child and part of the estate. Do you confess to the adultery, Baron Sprengel?

BARON: Yes, with regret and shame, but there are mitigating circumstances. I was forced into a state of humiliating celibacy through the Baroness's calculated frigidity, regardless of the fact that I only politely asked permission to gain through courtesy what the law grants me as a right; I grew tired of buying her love; she had introduced prostitution into my marriage by selling her favours first in exchange for power, then for gifts and money; and ultimately I found myself, and with the Baroness's explicit consent, forced to enter into a casual affair.

JUDGE: The Baroness had given her consent?

BARONESS: It's not true! I demand proof!

BARON: It's true, but I can't prove it since the only witness, my wife, is denying it!

JUDGE: Unproven isn't necessarily untrue, but an agreement of this nature, contrary to the law, is a *pactum turpe* and void. Baron Sprengel, the evidence is still stacked against you.

BARONESS: And since the Baron has admitted the crime with regret and shame, I ask that the Court proceed to the verdict as I'm now the plaintiff rather than the defendant and further details are unnecessary.

JUDGE: In my capacity as Chairman of the Court, I'd like to hear what the Baron has to say in his own defence or at least as justification.

BARON: I've admitted my adultery and brought up, as a mitigating circumstance, that it happened firstly out of compelling need, since I suddenly, after ten years of marriage, found myself a bachelor, and secondly because the Baroness had given her consent. However, as it now occurs to me that it may have been a ruse to build a case against me, it's my duty, for the sake of my son, to go further...

BARONESS *(exclaims involuntarily)*: Axel!

BARON: The cause of my adultery was the infidelity of the Baroness.

JUDGE: Can you prove that she was unfaithful, Baron Sprengel?

BARON: No! I was anxious to protect my family's honour, and so destroyed all the evidence I had, but I believe that the Baroness will stand by the confession she once made to me!

JUDGE: Baroness Sprengel, do you admit that your adultery preceded and thereby caused the Baron's indiscretion?

BARONESS: No!

JUDGE: Would you swear that you're innocent of this accusation?

BARONESS: Yes!

BARON: Dear Lord! No! She mustn't! No perjury for my sake!

JUDGE: I'll ask you once more: do you wish to swear the oath, Baroness Sprengel?

BARONESS: Yes!

BARON: I must stress that the Baroness is currently the plaintiff, and accusations are not made under oath.

JUDGE: As you've accused her of a crime, she's now the defendant. What does the Panel think?

EMANUEL WICKBERG: Since Baroness Sprengel is party to the case, she can hardly testify in her own defence, in my opinion.

SVEN OSKAR ERLIN: I think that if the Baroness gives evidence under oath, the Baron should also be allowed to do so, but since oath can't stand against oath the whole business seems muddled.

AUGUST ALEXANDER VASS: Surely this isn't a question of a witness oath, but a defensive oath.

ANDERS ERIK RUTH: That's clearly the question to settle first.

AXEL VALLIN: However, not in the presence of the parties, since the deliberations of the Court are not public.

KARL JOHAN SJÖBERG: A Magistrate's right to speak isn't limited by the condition of secrecy.

JUDGE: I can draw no guidance from such differing opinions. But since the Baron's crime can be proven, and the Baroness's remains unproven, I must require testimony under oath from the Baroness.

BARONESS: I'm ready!

JUDGE: No, wait. – Is it possible for the Baron, if granted an extension, to bring forward evidence or witnesses to support his accusation?

BARON: Even if I could, I wouldn't. I'm not inclined to expose my disgrace to the public.

JUDGE: The Court is now in recess while I seek the advice of the Chairman of the Parish Council. *(Leaves his chair and exits stage right).*

Scene Ten

LAY MAGISTRATES *(discussing amongst themselves half-audibly).* BARON and BARONESS *(upstage).* SPECTATORS *(talking in groups).*

BARON *(to the Baroness)*: You're not afraid of perjury?

BARONESS: I'm not afraid of anything when it comes to my child.

BARON: But if I have evidence?

BARONESS: You don't.

BARON: I burned the letters, but I have countersigned copies.

BARONESS: You're just saying that to frighten me.

BARON: To show you how deeply I love my child and to at least save its mother, since I myself am lost, I – here, take the evidence; but show some gratitude. *(Hands her a bundle of letters.)*

BARONESS: I always knew you were a liar, but I would never have believed that you were insidious enough to have the letters copied.

BARON: There's gratitude for you! Now we're both lost.

BARONESS: Yes, may we both be ruined, so there may be an end to this quarrel.

BARON: Would it be better for the child to lose both his parents and stand alone in the world?

BARONESS: That could never happen!

BARON: Your preposterous arrogance, which makes you believe that you stand above all laws and your fellow men, has fooled you into this struggle, in which one person is certain to lose: our son! What were you thinking when you began this attack, which must provoke a defence? It wasn't of the child! Was it revenge? Revenge for what? Because I uncovered your crime!

BARONESS: The child? Were you thinking of the child when you sullied me in front of this mob?

BARON: Hélène! – We've torn each other apart like savage beasts, we've revealed our shame in front of all these people who revel in our fall, because here, in this room, we don't have a single friend; from today our child won't be able to speak of honourable parents, nor count on a good word from his father and mother to help him in life; he'll see his home shunned and his ageing parents despised and alone until one day he'll flee from us!

BARONESS: So what do you want?

BARON: We'll go abroad once the estate is sold!

BARONESS: And start quarrelling all over again! I know how it goes: you'll be gentle for eight days, and then you'll turn vicious.

BARON: – Imagine, right now our destiny's being decided in there: You can't rely on a good word from the Pastor, whom you've just called a liar; nor can I expect any leniency as I'm known for my lack of Christian faith. Oh, I wish I could lie under the roots of a tree in the forest and hide my head under a rock – that's how ashamed I feel!

BARONESS: It's true, the Pastor hates us both, and what you say could happen. You speak to him!

BARON: About what? A reconciliation?

BARONESS: About whatever you please, as long as it's not too late! What if it's too late? What does this Alexandersson want, why does he keep prowling about? I fear that man!

BARON: Alexandersson's a decent chap!

BARONESS: Towards you, yes, but not towards me! – I've seen that look before! – Go to the Pastor now; but first hold my hand; I'm so afraid!

BARON: Of what, my dear, of what?

BARONESS: I don't know. – Everything, everyone!

BARON: But not of me, surely?

BARONESS: Not anymore! It's as if we're being pulled into some inexorable machine and our clothes are caught up in the gears. And all these wicked people are looking at us, laughing! – What have we done? What have we done in our anger? To think of the satisfaction they'll all get, seeing the Baron and Baroness undressed, abusing each other. – Oh, I feel as if I'm standing here naked. *(She buttons up her coat.)*

BARON: Calm down, my dear! This isn't the right place to tell you what I've told you before: that you have only one friend and one home, but we could start over! – – God knows! No, we can't. It's gone too far. It's over! And this final… yes, may it be the last! And it must follow from the rest! – No, we must be enemies as long as we live! And were I to release you now with the child, then you could remarry – I can see that now; and then my child would have a stepfather; and I would see my wife and son in the company of another man. – Or I myself might walk with someone else's harlot on my arm! No! – It's either you or me! One of us must be punished! You or me!

BARONESS: You! For if I let you go with the child, then you could remarry, and I would have to see another woman as mother to my child! Oh, the thought alone is enough to make a murderer of me! Stepmother to *my* child!

BARON: You should have thought about that earlier, but when you saw how I tore at the bonds of my love, which tied me to you, you thought I could never love anyone else.

BARONESS: Do you think I ever loved you?

BARON: Yes, at least once! When I was unfaithful to you! Then your love was sublime. And your feigned contempt made you irresistible. But my crime made you respect me too! I don't know whether it was the man or the criminal whom you admired the most, but I believe it was both, it must have been both, because you're the truest woman I've ever seen! You're already jealous of my potential wife. What a pity that you became my spouse! As my mistress your victory would have been uncontested and your infidelities would have been nothing more than the bouquet of my young wine.

BARONESS: Yes, your love was always sensual!

BARON: Sensual, like all things spiritual; spiritual like all things sensual! The depth of my passion was my weakness and it made you think that you were stronger, when you were only meaner, more brutal, more ruthless than I.

BARONESS: You, stronger! You don't want the same thing for two minutes; you don't even know what you want!

BARON: I do know full well what I want, but I can contain both love and hate, and I love you one minute and hate you the next! But now I hate you!

BARONESS: Are you thinking of our child now?

BARON: Yes, now as ever! And do you know why? Because he's our love incarnate. He's the memory of our affectionate moments, the bond that ties our souls together, the point where we inevitably meet. And this is why we'll never be able to part, even if our divorce is granted. – Oh, if only I could hate you the way I want to!

Scene Eleven

AS BEFORE. JUDGE and PASTOR *(Enter in conversation; stop downstage).*

JUDGE: I thus realise the utter futility of striving for fairness and seeking the truth. And it seems to me that the law's a few centuries behind our understanding of justice. Didn't

I just have to fine the innocent Alexandersson and restore the honour of a thieving maid? As regards this divorce case, at the moment I'm not certain of anything and so my conscience prevents me from reaching a verdict.

PASTOR: But a verdict must be reached!

JUDGE: Not by me! – I'll resign my office and seek a different career!

PASTOR: Oh! The scandal would only make you infamous and close all doors to you. Keep at it for a few years and you'll see that crushing people's lives like eggs will come more easily to you. Besides, if you wish to avoid responsibility in this case, then let the Magistrates' vote overrule yours, and they'll shoulder it for you.

JUDGE: That's a thought, and I believe they'll unite against me because I do have an opinion on this matter, though I daren't trust it since it's based on intuition – Thank you for the advice!

SHERIFF *(who has been talking to Alexandersson, approaches the Judge)*: As the prosecutor of this Court, I request permission to call Mr Alexandersson as a witness against Baroness Sprengel.

JUDGE: Regarding the adultery?

SHERIFF: Yes.

JUDGE *(to the Pastor)*: This could lead to a solution!

PASTOR: There are probably many leads, if only they can be found.

JUDGE: But isn't it horrible to see two people, who were once in love, destroy each other like this? It's like watching a massacre.

PASTOR: Well, that's love for you, your Honour.

JUDGE: Then what is hate?

PASTOR: It's the lining of the dress!

(The Judge goes to speak to the Magistrates.)

BARONESS *(approaches the Pastor)*: Help us, Pastor! Help us!

PASTOR: I can't and furthermore as a clergyman, I'm not allowed. Besides, didn't I warn you not to play with fire? – You thought getting a divorce was easy. So get one! The law's not stopping you; don't blame it.

Scene Twelve

AS BEFORE.

JUDGE: The Court is back in session! The public prosecutor, Sheriff Viberg, has informed the Court that a witness has come forward against the Baroness, confirming the breaking of her marriage vows. Mr Alexandersson!

ALEXANDERSSON: Present.

JUDGE: How can Mr Alexandersson prove his allegation?

ALEXANDERSSON: I saw the crime committed.

BARONESS: He lies! He'll have to prove it.

ALEXANDERSSON: Prove it? I'm only supposed to testify this time, aren't I?

BARONESS: Your accusation isn't proof, even if you're called a witness at the moment.

ALEXANDERSSON: Maybe the witness needs to have two witnesses, and those two witnesses two more each and so on?

BARONESS: Yes, that might be necessary when there's no way of knowing if they're all lying!

BARON: Alexandersson's testimony won't be needed. I ask the Court's permission to submit the correspondence which provides full evidence of Baroness Sprengel's adultery. – Here are the originals; copies can be found with the defendant.

(The Baroness lets out a scream, but recovers.)

JUDGE: But Baroness Sprengel was willing to take an oath just now?

BARONESS: But I didn't! – Besides, I think the Baron and I are even now.

JUDGE: One crime does not cancel out another; each person shall be held to account separately.

BARONESS: Then, while we're on that subject, I would like to sue Baron Sprengel for my dowry, which he has squandered.

JUDGE: If the Baron has squandered Baroness Sprengel's dowry, that matter should be settled now.

BARON: The Baroness brought with her into the marriage shares to a value of six thousand kronor, which were impossible to sell and soon became worthless. Since she had employment as a telegraph operator at the time of marriage, and declared that she didn't wish to be kept by her husband, we entered into a prenuptial agreement stipulating that each would support themselves. But after the wedding, she lost her position and since then I've supported her. I've never complained, but as she's now presenting me with a bill, I wish to present my counter-bill. It runs up to thirty-five thousand kronor, amounting to a third of the household's expenditure during our marriage, as I take two thirds upon myself.

JUDGE: Was the prenuptial agreement in writing, Baron Sprengel?

BARON: No.

JUDGE: Do you have any documentation relating to your dowry, Baroness Sprengel?

BARONESS: At the time I didn't think I'd need anything written down, since I assumed I was dealing with honest people!

JUDGE: Then I can't take the matter into consideration. – Would the Magistrates like to step into the next room to deliberate and reach a verdict?

Scene Thirteen

AS BEFORE. MAGISTRATES and JUDGE *(exit stage right)*.

ALEXANDERSSON *(to the Sheriff)*: I can't make head or tail of this justice.

SHERIFF: I think it would be advisable for you to go home now, or you may end up like that farmer from Mariestad. Ever heard of him?

ALEXANDERSSON: No.

SHERIFF: Well! He went to court out of pure curiosity; was

dragged into the case as a witness, became a party to it and ended up being sentenced to twenty lashes!

ALEXANDERSSON: Bloody hell! But I can believe it of them! I believe they're capable of anything! *(Exits.)*

BARON *(approaches the Baroness downstage.)*

BARONESS: You're finding it hard being away from me?

BARON: Hélène! I've stabbed you, but I'm the one bleeding to death, for your blood is mine…

BARONESS: And how well you write bills!

BARON: No, only counter-bills! Your courage is born out of a desperation with no room for hope. When you leave this courtroom, you'll collapse. You'll no longer have me to pile grief and guilt upon, and your conscience will devour you. Do you know why I haven't killed myself?

BARONESS: You're scared!

BARON: Yes! Not of eternal damnation – I don't believe in that – but because I know that even if you get the child, you'll be dead in five years time, the doctor has told me so: and then the child will have neither father nor mother. Imagine: all alone in the world!

BARONESS: Five years! – That's a lie!

BARON: Five years. Then the child will be mine whether you like it or not.

BARONESS: Oh no! My family will sue to take the child away from you! I don't die when I die!

BARON: Wickedness never dies! That's true. – But can you explain to me why you begrudge me the child, and the child his father, whom he needs? Are you punishing the child out of sheer cruelty and vengefulness?

BARONESS *(is silent.)*

BARON: I once told the Pastor that I believed you had doubts about the child's paternity, and that this was why you wouldn't leave the child with me, so that I wouldn't build my happiness on false grounds. To which he replied: No, I don't think she would have such a noble motive. Personally, I don't think you understand why you're so fanatical about this, but what compels us to cling to our children is our desire to live on in them. Our son has your body, but my soul and you can't purge that. You'll see me reappear in him when you least expect it: you'll see my thoughts, my inclinations, my passions in him, and one day you'll hate him like you hate me! This is what I fear!

BARONESS: It seems you're still afraid that he will be mine!

BARON: Being a mother and a woman gives you an advantage over me in the eyes of these judges; justice may indeed play dice blindfolded, but the dice are always loaded.

BARONESS: Even at the brink of divorce you're all politeness; perhaps you don't hate me as much as you pretend to?

BARON: To be honest, I think I hate my disgrace more than I hate you, though I do that, too. And why this hideous hatred? Perhaps I've forgotten that you're nearing your fortieth year, and that a man is developing within you. Perhaps it's this man whom I've noticed in your kisses, in your embraces, and who's so repulsive to me!

BARONESS: Perhaps! You never knew that the great tragedy of my life is that I wasn't born a man.

BARON: Perhaps it became the great tragedy of my life! And now you're taking revenge on nature's trick by raising your son a woman. Will you promise me something?

BARONESS: Will *you* promise me something?

BARON: What good is promising? We never keep our promises anyway!

BARONESS: No! Let's promise no more!

BARON: Will you answer one question truthfully?

BARONESS: Even if I told the truth, you'd think I was lying.

BARON: Yes, I would!

BARONESS: Do you see now that it's over, forever!

BARON: Forever! Forever – as we once vowed to love one another?

BARONESS: How terrible to be forced to vow such a thing!

BARON: Why? It's a bond after all, such as it is.

BARONESS: I could bear no bondage.

BARON: Do you think it would have been better if we hadn't married?

BARONESS: For me, yes.

BARON: I wonder! Then you would have had no hold on me.

BARONESS: Or you, on me.

BARON: So the result would have been just the same – like a reduced fraction. To sum up: It's not the law's fault, not our fault, nor the fault of others! And yet we are to bear the blame! *(the Sheriff approaches.)* So. The verdict has been reached. – Good-bye Hélène!

BARONESS: Good-bye! – Axel!

BARON: It's hard to part! And impossible to live together. But at least the struggle's over!

BARONESS: If only it were! – I fear it's only just beginning!

SHERIFF: Would the parties please leave while the Court deliberates.

BARONESS: Axel! One more word before it's too late! It's possible that they'll take the child from both of us, isn't it? So go home and take the boy to your mother, and then we'll flee far, far away!

BARON: I think you're trying to fool me again!

BARONESS: No, I'm not. I'm not thinking of you any more, nor of myself, nor of my revenge. Just save the child! Do you hear me! Do it!

BARON: I'll do it! But if you've tricked me… Very well: I'll do it! *(Exits quickly.)*

BARONESS *(exits through the door upstage).*

Scene Fourteen

LAY MAGISTRATES and JUDGE *(enter and take their places).*

JUDGE: As our deliberations have been concluded, I would ask the Magistrates to express their opinions before the verdict is pronounced. As far as I'm concerned it seems reasonable to award the mother custody as both spouses are equally to blame for the divorce and the mother must be considered more naturally inclined to care for the child than the father. *(Silence.)*

ALEXANDER EKLUND: According to the law the wife takes the husband's social position and conditions in life and not the reverse.

EMANUEL WICKBERG: And the husband is rightly the wife's protector!

KARL JOHAN SJÖBERG: In the marriage contract, which, after all, legitimises the marriage, the wife is bid to submit to her husband, from which I believe it clearly follows that the man comes before the woman.

ERIK OTTO BOMAN: And the children must be raised in the father's faith.

ERENFRID SÖDERBERG: From which it's also clear that children follow the father and not the mother.

OLOF ANDERSSON: But in the present case the spouses are equally criminal, and, given everything that has been brought to light, equally unsuited to raising a child. I say that the child should be taken from both of them.

KARL PETER ANDERSSON: I agree with Olof Andersson and I recall that in such cases the judge will appoint two trustees to administer the estate and to allocate part of its annual income as an allowance for the child's foster parents.

AXEL VALLIN: Then I would like to suggest as trustees Alexander Eklund and Erenfrid Söderberg, who are both known for their dependable character and Christian disposition.

ANDERS ERIK RUTH: I agree with Olof Andersson of Vik, regarding the separation of the child from both father and mother and with Axel Vallin regarding the trustees, whose Christian temper makes them particularly suited for being responsible for the child.

SVEN OSKAR ERLING: I agree with the previous speaker.

AUGUST ALEXANDER VASS: Agreed.

LUDVIG ÖSTMAN: Agreed.

JUDGE: Since the Magistrates' opinions seem to be the opposite of mine, I ask you to proceed to a vote. Perhaps I may suggest that the motion be Olof Andersson's proposal to separate the child from both father and mother and appoint trustees. Is this the unanimous decision of the Panel?

MAGISTRATES: Yes!

JUDGE: If anyone opposes the motion, please raise your hand now. *(Pause.)* The opinion of the Panel has thus prevailed over my own, and I would like the record to reflect my reservations about what seems to me an overly harsh sentence. – The Court orders the spouses to complete one year's separation of bed and residence on pain of imprisonment should they seek each other during this time. *(To the Sheriff)* Call in the parties!

Scene Fifteen

AS BEFORE. BARONESS. SPECTATORS *(enter)*.

JUDGE: Is Baron Sprengel absent?

BARONESS: The Baron will be here shortly.

JUDGE: He who is tardy has only himself to blame. – The verdict of the Court is as follows: Baron and Baroness Sprengel are ordered to separate for one year; the child will be taken from its parents and assigned two trustees, for which duty the Court has appointed the Lay Magistrates Alexander Eklund and Erenfrid Söderberg.

(The Baroness screams and falls. The Sheriff and Constable lift her up and help her to a chair. Some of the spectators begin to leave.)

BARON *(enters)*: Your Honour! Having heard the verdict of the Court from outside, I wish to challenge the impartiality of the Magistrates, who are all my personal enemies, and also the suitability of Alexander Eklund and Erenfrid Söderberg, neither of whom possesses the financial security required of trustees; furthermore I intend to file a suit against the Judge for incompetence in the exercise of his office, since he failed to recognise that the party who began breaking up the marriage is the cause of the other's breaking, and that therefore both can't be equally guilty.

JUDGE: Anyone not satisfied with the verdict must make their case to the Court of Appeal within the prescribed time limits! The Court will proceed to inspect the parsonage in connection with the next case, against the valuers from the County Council.

JUDGE and MAGISTRATES *(exit upstage.)*

Scene sixteen

BARON. BARONESS. SPECTATORS *(exit)*.

BARONESS *(gets up)*: Where's Emile?
BARON: He was gone!
BARONESS: You're lying!
BARON *(after a pause)*: Yes. – I decided not to take him to my mother because I don't trust her, but to the parsonage instead.
BARONESS: To the Pastor!
BARON: Your only reliable enemy! Yes! Who else would I dare trust! And I did it because I caught a look in your eye just now and it told me that you might kill yourself and the child.
BARONESS: Really? You saw that. – Oh, that I allowed myself to be fooled into trusting you.
BARON: So, what do you make of this?
BARONESS: I don't know; I'm so weary I no longer feel anything. Rather, it seems a relief to have been dealt the deathblow.
BARON: You're not thinking of the consequences: your son will be raised by two peasants whose ignorance and simple habits will slowly torment him to death; he'll be forced down into their confined sphere; his intelligence will be suffocated by religious superstition; he'll be taught to despise his parents…
BARONESS: Quiet! Don't say any more; I'm losing my mind! My Emile amongst peasant wives, who don't wash, who have bedbugs and can't tell whether a comb is clean! My Emile? No, it's not possible!
BARON: It's happening and you've no one but yourself to blame!
BARONESS: Myself! Yes, but did I create myself? Instill wicked inclinations or sow hatred and wild passions in myself? No!

Who denied me the strength and the will to fight them? When I look at myself right now, I think I deserve to be pitied! Don't you?

BARON: Yes! We both deserve to be pitied! We tried to avoid the pitfalls of marriage and live together as husband and wife without being married; but we still fought, didn't we? And we had forfeited one of life's greatest pleasures: the esteem of others. So we got married. But we tried to out-wit society and its laws; we wouldn't have a church wedding, instead we wriggled our way into a civil marriage; we wouldn't depend on one another... not share our money, not insist upon ownership of the other person – and yet it was the same old story! No church wedding, but a prenuptial agreement! And then it broke! I forgave your infidelity and for the sake of the child we privately agreed to free one another from our vows – some freedom! But I grew tired of introducing my friend's mistress as my wife – and so we had to get divorced! Do you know what? Do you know what we've been fighting? You call him God, but I call him nature! And this tyrant stirred our hatred of each other, just as he induces people to fall in love. And now we're condemned to rip each other apart for as long as there's a spark of life left in us. New cases in the Court of Appeal, repeated rejections of our case, the hearings of the Parish Council, the verdict of the clergy, the verdict of the Supreme Court! Then comes my appeal to the Department of Justice, my application for new trustees, your challenges and counter-suits: from scaffold to scaffold! Without ever finding a compassionate executioner! – The mismanagement of the estate, financial ruin, our child's upbringing neglected! And why don't we end these two miserable lives? Because the child prevents us! – You're crying, but I can't! Not even when I think of the night which awaits me in our desolate home! And you, poor Hélène, you'll go back to your mother! Your mother, whom you left with a light heart to build your own home! Become her daughter again... that might be worse than being a wife! – One year! Two years! Several years! How many more

do you think we can endure?
BARONESS: I'll never go back to my mother! Never! I'll take to the roads and forests to hide myself and to shout, shout myself hoarse at God, who allowed infernal love into this world to torment us. And when darkness falls I'll lie down in the parsonage's barn to sleep near to my child.
BARON: You'll sleep tonight, will you?

Curtain

Translators' Note

The Bond is the longest play in this collection and has by far the most characters on stage, no less than twenty-four in all. It is a complex text which incorporates many of the broad themes Strindberg returned to throughout his career, themes such as gender, the possibility of lasting love, class and the struggle of individuals against social systems and norms.

In order to do Strindberg and the play justice, our foremost aim when translating was to retain the many-layered structure and multifaceted characters of the original, thus leaving as many opportunities for interpretation as possible open to the reader or performer.

Over-interpretation of the characters was an ever present danger; Strindberg seems to invite readings focused on specific aspects, particularly gender and class, and at times the temptation to simplify can be overwhelming for both reader and translator. We have done our best to produce a translation that lets the characters speak for themselves, while preserving the antinomies that doubtlessly exist in the text: between men and women, between lower and higher class and between individual will and the forces of society. Our hope is that this will allow the reader to discover not only how modern this play still remains but also how funny it can be. No one is spared, no one idealised; this is a vision of real men and women, all flawed, participating in a ritual as old as human relationships – in which everyone ends up a loser. Strindberg's creation certainly is bleak but also permeated by a biting sense of humour.

From the outset we have been committed to staying close to Strindberg's language, but it is difficult to know what "staying close" means when dealing with a text written in 1892, which to make matters worse, incorporates a lot of legal and idiomatic terminology. We soon rejected the idea of trying to mimic English of the 1890's, but rather took our cue from Strindberg's own habit of writing in a modern mode, feeling free to adopt the dialogue to a contemporary English-speaking audience. For instance, in translating the titles of the court officials we looked for English words that give an intuitive understanding of their social status and role in the community rather turning to historical records in search of contemporary equivalents. Likewise, we tried to phrase specifically Swedish cultural practices in more general terms to avoid the need for footnotes or explanations.

We felt that this was important considering that the plays are meant to be usable as the basis of performances; overly archaic language would only be a barrier for both the actors and the audience. On the other hand, we had no desire to turn the translation into 21st century colloquial English, feeling that this would be a step too far in terms of style and, moreover, that it was unnecessary in order to convey the modernity of the play.

In our wish to stay close to the original text we have also been careful to reproduce the structural and stylistic devices, big and small, with which Strindberg peppered this play and which carry significant symbolic and thematic weight. These range from the structurally fundamental, such as the doubling of the two court cases and the frequently repeated pairing of characters, to the linguistically specific, such as recurring metaphors and key expressions.

Even with the best of intentions, however, translation necessarily entails interpreting the original and inevitably the translation before you reflects our points of view as much as it does Strindberg's. But we have done our best to locate and reproduce, rather than resolve, the ambiguities of the text. We have tried to understand the different mental states of the characters, reading almost every speech alternatingly with anger, vehemence, sarcasm, sadness or spite, reminding ourselves constantly that in *The Bond*, as in real life, everyone is both victim and villain, shallow and profound, dissembling and sincere. In setting down the English text we wanted to make sure that all possible readings and emotions would remain latent in the play, so that the English reader may discover the same compelling complexity as we did in reading Strindberg's original.

Agnes Broomé and Mathelinda Nabugodi

AUGUST STRINDBERG

The People of Hemsö

(translated by Peter Graves)

August Strindberg (1849-1912), Sweden's internationally recognised dramatist, was an astonishingly prolific all-rounder. The new National Edition of his works will run to seventy-two volumes: he was a writer of novels, short stories, essays, journalism and satire, he experimented with early photography, and in recent years his paintings have achieved the recognition they deserve.

His novel *The People of Hemsö* (1887) will come as a surprise to most English-language readers, used as they are to seeing the bitter controversialist of plays like *The Father* and *Miss Julie* or the seeker for cosmic meaning and reconciliation of those mysterious later dream plays *To Damascus* and *A Dream Play*. This novel, a tragicomic story of lust, love and death among the fishermen and farmers of the islands of the Stockholm Archipelago, reveals a very different Strindberg. The vigour and humour of the narration, as well as its cinematic qualities, are such that we witness a great series of peopled panoramas in which place and time and character are somehow simultaneously specific and archetypical, and we leave the novel with memories of grand landscapes and spirited scenes. In a recent essay Ludvig Rasmusson wrote: 'For me, *The People of Hemsö* is the Great Swedish Novel, just as ... *The Adventures of Huckleberry Finn* [is] the Great American Novel'. His comparison is an apt one: if the Mississippi becomes the quintessence of America, the island of Hemsö and the archipelago become the quintessence of Sweden.

ISBN 9781870041959
UK £11.95
(Paperback, 164 pages)